Happy

WE ARE THE PEOPLE

+ Sylvia!

I really enjoyed this exhibition at the National Portrait Gallery. I hope you have fun delving into it!

Love, Steve Jan Nia Liam, Paj + Cait
x x x x x x

P.S. Will you spot someone or somewhere familiar?

WE ARE THE PEOPLE

POSTCARDS FROM THE COLLECTION OF TOM PHILLIPS

Preface by James Fenton
Essay by Elizabeth Edwards

NATIONAL PORTRAIT GALLERY

The book was blue and somehow padded with the words Postcard Album deeply embossed on the cover. As Vellinger slowly turned its gilt-edged pages Rima saw women in vast improbable hats and men whose high and rigid collars must have bitten into their chins. A sequence of stiffly posed couples suddenly gave way to a double page of infants even more complicatedly dressed.

'What a sweet little girl!' said Rima, pointing at one almost smothered in dark velvet and a blizzard of intricate lace. Grenville laughed.

'Well,' he said, 'that little girl is the person you have just agreed to marry. And that is my sister on the other page with her doll. In those days boys and girls were dressed the same. I was very cross because I wasn't allowed to bring my toy boat. The photographer gave me a silly cloth dog to hold. That must have been the only smile they prised out of me that day. But how strange it is that before my parents, whose photographs you were just looking at, I have no pictures of more distant relatives, unless, that is, you count paintings of Adam and Eve...'

H.W.K. Collam,
from *Come Autumn Hand*, chapter 11

To Sir David Scholey, Chairman, and my fellow Trustees
of the National Portrait Gallery, London, for their kindness and support.

Published in Great Britain by National Portrait Gallery Publications,
National Portrait Gallery, St Martin's Place, London WC2H 0HE

To accompany the exhibition *We Are The People: Postcards from the Collection of Tom Phillips* at the National Portrait Gallery
2 March – 20 June 2004

For a complete catalogue of current publications, please write to
the address above, or visit our website at www.npg.org.uk

ISBN 1 85514 517 0

A catalogue record for this book is available from the British Library.

Publications Manager: Denny Hemming
Production: Ruth Müller-Wirth
Design: Price Watkins Design
Printed in Italy

Front and back cover: Collection of Tom Phillips

Contents

Foreword

PHOTOGRAPHS of unknown sitters are intriguing. Anonymous to the viewer now, and disconnected from all that linked them to a place, to a family or to a friend, their faces look confidently out, knowing full well who they are. Despite that original confidence, postcard portraits have generally been discarded: thrown out into clearance sales, dropped from the letters or messages with which they were sent, or slipped from the albums where they might have remained labelled and known.

Their very anonymity is poignant, offering a Proust-like savouring of memory, as if a postcard could act as the smell or taste of a past to be recovered. Each image is a suspended moment, presented for our contemplation: Who is this? What life did they lead? Where was the photograph taken, and why?

People are mostly not at work in these images; many have dressed and posed for their portraits so that future generations can see them at their best. And their settings are often suggestive of a world becoming modern. As Tom Phillips observes in his introduction, the photographic postcards together make an alternate National Portrait Gallery, no longer focused on national achievement and eminence, but rather on the people whose daily activities make a society, an economy and a culture.

Tom Phillips has been collecting photographic postcards for many years, searching through antique shops, jumble sales and postcard fairs to select those that have a striking or telling image. His fascination and determination are hugely to our benefit. And the categories of his own devising represent the artist-curator's natural instinct to put things in piles – in boxes or folders – or at least in some kind of order. But the groupings give us as spectators the ability to make sense of the images, despite their anonymity. They provide a new context for exhibiting his selection of around a thousand images of people from the first five decades of the twentieth century.

I am very grateful to James Fenton and to Elizabeth Edwards for their excellent contributions to this book, published to accompany the exhibition. I also extend thanks to Denny Hemming for her editorial expertise, to Price-Watkins who have undertaken the book design, to Sophie Clark for her managerial work on the exhibition, and to Ian Gardner for overseeing its design. I also wish to acknowledge the work of the Trading and Publishing department, the Development and Communications department, and the Education department, all of which has been essential in realising both the exhibition and the book.

Finally I wish to thank Tom Phillips who has worked tirelessly, selecting the postcards, working closely on all aspects of the design, and always giving the project his full attention in a busy schedule. We are very grateful to him.

Sandy Nairne
Director, National Portrait Gallery

Preface: Collecting Postcards
James Fenton

T HEY are an invention, like the postage stamp. So they have a beginning in history, and they have an end, like the telegram, the *petit bleu*, the *carte de visite*, the message in the cleft stick. Like the *ostrakon*, the lead tablet at the buried spring, with its scratched imprecation or common abuse, like the impression of gold in hot sealing wax, like all the technology of the wedding video, like the hand outlined in ochre on the cave wall (where would you find the ochre? where would you find the cave?) – but unlike the letter, unlike the portrait, the self-portrait, unlike the signature. Unlike any of those simple gestures by which one being says to another: I was here.

I saw this patch of cement drying on the pavement, and I signed it. I came to this temple, and I happened to have my chisel in my pocket. Your van was filthy dirty, so I wrote a message on it, divulging something unreliable about your private life....

Such messages are the product of a momentary exuberance, and their recipient is an imaginary public, whereas these postcards are the considered record of a moment, and all their recipients were known to the senders.

Hello. It's me. It's us. This is the spot on the mountain, this is the boarding-house room, this is the sea front. We got here. We made it. Don't you wish you had made it with us? Don't you wish you were here?

The technology dies. The desire persists. It wanders on and finds a new technology. Years later, looking back on this humblest kind of memento, we find that it begins to speak to us in a new way, as from an irrecoverable world. The first meaning it had has long since been forgotten. Now it has a new meaning. It has become a collectable.

There are two kinds of collecting: the selective and the accumulative. In the first, the collector seeks to assemble only the best examples of a class of object (paintings, sculptures, porcelain). The collection improves as its quality, but not its quantity, increases. With this method, sacrifices may continually be made, as objects of lesser worth are sold to help with the acquisition of more desirable items. The number of entries in the inventory may remain static over the years, but the collection is seen to advance through substitution, or through a process of 'trading up'.

Pepys's Library – the one for which he had made the first-known purposely-built bookcases in England – was intended to comprise 'in fewest Books and least Room the greatest diversity of Subjects, Stiles, and Languages its Owner's Reading [would] bear'. Three thousand volumes was the target, in twelve bookcases. When Pepys acquired a superior version of a book, he discarded what was inferior. If he read a book he didn't like, he got rid of it. He always kept a sense of scale.

In the second, accumulative type of collection, the significance of the individual object is seen to grow through the fact of its keeping company with such a large number of items of a similar kind: one Gabon stamp may be neither here nor there, but fifty Gabon stamps act as a spur to the acquisition of fifty more. And as the ceiling is reached, as all the Gabon stamps seem to have been tracked down, a kind of restlessness sets in – Cameroon suddenly becomes interesting and desirable from the collector's point of view. Soon it is no longer a matter of forming a collection. Multiple classes of object have begun to occupy the collector's attention.

A formidable representative of this cast of mind was the tenor Evangelista Gorga (Rodolfo in the 1896 Turin premier of *La Bohème*), who in 1899 retired early from the stage in order to devote himself to his collections in Rome, which occupied the remainder of his long life (1865–1957). He was a connoisseur of musical instruments (he had about as many instruments as Pepys had books). He collected ancient arms, fossils and toys of all epochs, medical equipment and surgical instruments, tools of all trades and professions, as well as bronzes, terracottas and objects in ivory or bone, until he had thirty distinct collections comprising a total of 150,000 items.

To house these he rented ten apartments in the same building (285 via Cola di Rienzo), where the thirty collections were installed without inventory or catalogue: the tobacco museum, with its pipes, pouches and cigar cases; the prints and drawings; the coloured marbles; toilet items from all ages; the health museum, itself including some twenty pharmacies from periods between 1000BC and the nineteenth century; the inscriptions; the artistic and scientific library, ancient and modern; the Risorgimento collection; the cookery equipment of every epoch.

Before too long he was bankrupt and his collections under sequestration by the State. But he had done some good with all his mania, and some of his collections still exist, for public benefit and pleasure.

And it is right to say that this kind of accumulation has a point. The significance of a jar is indeed brought out by its correct placing in a pharmacy. The significance of a pharmacy is indeed enhanced by the comparison – if such could ever be achieved – with twenty other pharmacies down the ages. One might contend that it was wrong of Gorga to rent ten apartments (to make a collection of apartments), when it must surely have been cheaper to buy a whole building. But that is a rather prosaic argument to put up against the encyclopaedic vision of the collector, one of whose categories comprised *oggetti di tutto lo scibile, dall' arcaico ai tempi nostri* – objects of all knowledge, from archaic times to our own.

Flinders Petrie, the great Egyptologist, had a plan for a museum that would have solved Evan Gorga's problem. He wanted a large tract of land to be purchased somewhere in the Home Counties, on which would be placed a simple modular structure, sufficient to hold the museum's collections as they then were. In due course, if, as was likely, Assyria yielded up some great wealth of treasure, a further module would be added to the museum, to accommodate the finds. If cartloads of carvings arrived from Africa, a corresponding department could be extended along lines already envisaged. Ordering a new wing to be built, in this vision, would be simplicity itself; the whole kit might be sitting there, ready for assembly. I imagine that Petrie had in mind some kind of pattern like a snowflake crystal, which would simply grow and grow until that patch of the Home Counties was museumed over.

Collections of such a character need space. Alternatively, one may choose to collect objects that are by nature modest in their requirements. Even Pepys, within his carefully scaled library, had volumes of prints, and a collection of broadside ballads – accumulative collections within his selective framework. And we will always be grateful to those snappers-up of ephemera who thought of saving what was in their own day disprized – those who in our times, for instance, have been keeping track of the prostitutes' cards that have littered the telephone booths of London.

To such pioneers, such archivists of the obvious, there is nothing that cannot be collected. The trick is to think of the category… and then to persist. Two such collectors, in an article I read not long ago, were driving on their way to make a purchase when one stopped the car and approached a hitchhiker, offering him $25 for his cardboard sign. On the spur of the moment, he had conceived the plan to make a collection of hitchhikers' cardboard signs.

The example illustrates the paradigm. The individual object is of no great worth or interest on its own. It is only through accumulation, only by becoming one of a category, that it has any great chance of engaging our interest. And this particular case seems particularly unpromising. But one has to remember that all such ephemera, by definition, must once have seemed unpromising. The Wanted poster from the Wild West, which today would be such a find, or the printed advertisement for the slave auction, were once trash.

Astonishingly common things have a way of becoming astonishingly rare. For instance, the pious Victorians who printed and handed out tracts by the thousand, reckoning their own missions in terms of mass production, were creating a class of object that would become transcendentally scarce. I have seen many a papyrus from the ancient world, but I am not entirely sure that I have ever seen a real Victorian tract, and those scholars who work in this field are apparently hampered by the fact that the British Library's tract collection was destroyed by bombing in the Second World War.

But these postcards are not rare. They never were. They were made to be treasured by those directly involved in them – not for a moment by anyone else. But they were made in such quantities that, when they lost the significance, when their sitters died and their identities were in due course forgotten, still, by their sheer numbers and by the fact of their not being bulky, they could pass through a period of valuelessness into a new life as objects of curiosity.

So much that we admire today has passed through that period of disregard, that dangerous prelude to value. I remember in my childhood how the provincial auction rooms were filled with passed-over lots, those rosewood writing-cases that opened out to form a desk top. They seemed beautiful to me then, with their brassbound corners and their mother-of-pearl inlays, their square inkbottles and their 'secret drawers', but they were a drug on the market, and the auctioneers despised them almost as much as they despised pianos.

I think of them sometimes as I throw out yet another fax machine, or wonder if I will ever really use a typewriter again. Will people say of me and mine: they threw out their fax machines, just as their ancestors threw out their harpsichords?

Once they meant so much. Then they meant nothing. Then taste and curiosity took pity on them, and they began to mean something again. And so people began collecting these postcard portraits, these seaside souvenirs. And Tom Phillips, who made this research, these purchases, tells us he has assembled 50,000 cards, and sorted them into 120 categories, of which he offers us this wonderfully eloquent sample.

And we see here the strength of the accumulative method, for the categories do indeed come as a surprise. Who would have predicted that the aspidistra (which we remember only as a joke) would be such an important prop as to establish its own genre? Who could have foreseen the interest provided by the multiple views of the office or classroom?

What we could well have predicted, though, is the principal source of interest: a chapter in the history of self-presentation, as defined through a given technology, in a period normally delineated by the two great wars. We are warned by our collector/curator not to expect to be able to date these postcards accurately, and he is right, I think, to discourage the desire to define too accurately our feelings about what we are seeing. It is what we find elusive that keeps us happy wandering through this postcard museum, this exorbitant accumulation of lost selves.

Introduction
Tom Phillips

fig.1

THESE two young women seventy years ago are strolling past post-cards very like the one they are in. They may even *be* in one of the cards on display since these include the photos taken the day before from this same spot in Margate, which might well lie on their route from boarding house to beach. Tomorrow in any case they will be able to buy this cheerful image of themselves; and indeed that is what they did.

We are sometime in the early 1930s, though handbag or hair historians and experts on shoe styles should be able to pinpoint the exact year. Both women are of that first and last generation whose whole lives will have been marked out by postcard portraits. All being well (and conventional) their wedding photographs will coincide with the fading of the era in which everyone became a postcard.

As well as being one of that day's victims of the representative of Sunbeam Photo Ltd they will also have been the subject of more formal pictures. Each of them would have started in babyhood with involuntary attendance at the local photographer's studio, brought by her mother and carefully set down in christening finery or held up in a classic emblematic pose. The next postcard to place in an album or on the mantelpiece might have been two or three years later as an infant. Perhaps she is now dressed as a miniature adult or pinafored like the doll she is carrying as she stands before a painted backcloth that evokes a lyric world. School would bring its own portraiture, of her class or of herself as prizewinner in an event. As an early teenager (though teenagers had not yet been invented) there would be a photo with her father dressed in uniform ready to go out to fight in the First World War. The whole family might be gathered in the hope that this would not (as tragically it so often did) become 'the last time we were all together'; a standard image of the period (*fig.2*).

fig.2

Religion perhaps may have made an appearance by way of a first communion card (*fig.3*), or the burgeoning youth movements in the form of a proud and newly kitted-out Girl Guide. Beyond this the paths might fork as the young women take up different jobs in shop or office or mill and are captured on a postcard in the context of their work.

Thus one might hazard that each would, by the time we see them here in this impromptu portrait, have as many as a dozen likenesses of themselves. If a member of the family had been a keen amateur photographer there would be more, representing picnics or garden moments (for only the most ambitious would have tried their hand at indoor settings). As can be seen, however, one of them is carrying what must be a Box Brownie camera (Kodak's democratising equivalent of the Model T Ford) which itself will be the source of further images, blurry perhaps but still evocative of this seaside episode in lives we know so little about, for we are unaware of their relationship to each other as sisters, long-term friends, workmates, mere holiday acquaintances or even lovers. Such snaps with their typical postcard backs might themselves have qualified for this project for, by the mid twentieth century, not only had everyone become a postcard but almost all had become a photographer.

fig.3

fig.4

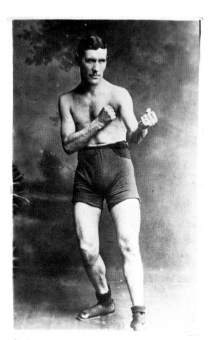

fig.5

The aesthetic of the picture is definitively vernacular, one might say even anarchic, dismissing as it does all the niceties and canonical correctnesses of the formal portrait and liberating the photograph from its long debt to painting. The photographer here is indifferent to the half-concealed figure of a man carrying a raincoat or the dying deck chair and leaves only the few ill-fitting boards of the walkway to give foreground interest. The hurriedly scratched code number (made on the negative via a small window in the camera) completes the impression of pictorial laissez faire.

Yet this very casualness exemplifies an aesthetic shared by another form of seaside artefact, the saucy postcard as made famous by the cunning and economical artistry of Donald McGill. It would not be difficult to adapt this composition into a typical comic card, with imagined dialogue as the caption and with just enough background detail to give it a context of place and weather.

This new aesthetic reflects the national story our project rehearses. It signals a general emancipation from restricted life, an abandonment of received criteria, a rejection of past values of dress and deportment as well as the imprisoning views of gender. Photographer and subjects collude unconsciously in a bid for freedom. Even though human beings by their nature can only escape from one prison to find themselves in another there can be a kind of progress in finding ampler cells and larger air.

Our project, as will appear in this and any subsequent selections, coincides with (and provides an analogue to) a social revolution as large and radical as any that took place amidst blood and ideological fanaticism elsewhere.

One only has to think of two women passing this spot a quarter of a century before and the striking contrast the pair of pictures would exhibit (and then to imagine the same set-up a quarter of a century later where one would notice less significant change) to appreciate the speed and size of that social upheaval. It may be that these very images were prime tools in that revolution and that it was the novel possibility of the mass of the people being not only visible to others but being able to see themselves that provided the insights and critique that made such a transformation possible.

The picture that provoked these reflections is in no way special and was merely chosen because of its intriguing combination of postcards within a postcard. In all other respects it is, in a phrase which itself can gather resonance through such images, deeply inconsequential. It could merge unremarked into the category of *Two Women: Actuality* (p.261) or a large group called *Promenade*.

Both women are approximately of my mother's generation since she was born only a year before the liberation of the postcard itself in 1902 (when the Post Office finally allowed written messages on the back of cards leaving the whole front free for pictorial matter). The picture here of my mother (*fig.4*) also dates from the beginning of the 1930s and serves to demonstrate, by way of contrast, the durability of the classic studio portrait and formal pose. I am glad to smuggle it in at this juncture since, had it been plucked from an anonymous pile, it would have been sorted under the heading *Dogs*.

My mother knew of no photographs of either of her parents, which emphasises the typical darkness that for most people existed before the advent of the postcard portrait. Its immediate predecessors, the ornately mounted cabinet picture and the smaller *carte de visite*, were widely available from the 1860s, yet were not only more expensive but seemed somehow to call for a greater investment of self esteem than the unpretentious unmounted card with postcard back.

My father was twenty years older than my mother and had posed for postcard images at more than one prime epoch of his life. That contemporary with my mother's picture shows him as a blandly pensive yet determined businessman but this much earlier card of him (*fig.5*) *circa* 1906 sees him in his heyday as a welterweight boxer. It would certainly be a candidate in its iconic purity for the *Sport* section of this book. His family too seems to disappear from view before the dawn of the twentieth century.

fig.6

Similarly the majority of mature people pictured here are the first in their familial histories to have been portrayed in any way at all. As Collam put it this was the time when 'a whole nation stepped into the light'. Elderly relatives were naturally brought into the visual round up and there is a whole category under the heading *Generations* featuring family groups in which three or even four generations are present. The oldest person, certainly the earliest born that I have in my collection, is stated on a card produced in 1904 to be 109 years old (*fig.6*) and therefore saw the end of the eighteenth century. The most recently born are often younger than myself and are perhaps as I write taking photos with digital cameras of their children; children who may live to see (if there is one) the twenty-second century.

But these of course would not be postcard portraits of the type whose life and slow demise is chronicled in this project. *We Are The People*, of which this book presents some sample fragments, has the ambition of being a visual epic of trivial fond record. What Hamlet is about to wipe from the table of his memory this project is committed to rescue. Perhaps the enterprise as a whole already stretches beyond the bounds of publishability since each of its categories could now occupy a whole volume. Its topics range from *Accessories* to *Windows* via *Caravans*, *Hats*, *Interiors*, *May Queens*, *Teddy Bears* etc. etc. Each embraces only those cards printed directly on to photographic stock with postcard backs, which are referred to in the world of deltiology (to use America's fancy name for postcard collecting) as Real Photo Postcards.

The decline in currency of such cards begins just before the Second World War. Wartime restrictions and economies certainly led to a quantitative dip, though the public unavailability of any new developments in stock or equipment may have prolonged the actual death throes. Certainly by 1950 only the odd professional attending provincial weddings and the few

fig.7

fig.8

residual seaside photographers competing with people armed with their own cameras were still active. There was I remember a postcard photographer in London who, on the windy concourses of the Festival of Britain in 1951, still plied his trade amongst the symbols of progress.

It was the first third of the century that saw the greatest concentration of cards, a period described in the postcard world as The Golden Age, a suspect term in any field which usually designates a period forever in the past which no one at the time was aware of experiencing. In those years the portrait photographer was multiply present in every town. Even villages, as is attested by the names of studios printed or embossed on so many cards, could boast one.

Arrived at a studio there was a choice of scenic backdrops that afforded comforting fictions in the form of surroundings you might not normally aspire to. These ranged from the platonic pastoral (with its echoes of painting's tradition of the Sublime) to poetic evocations of baronial splendour as you leaned on a hollow plaster balustrade or sat among marble pillars, gilded panelling and heavy drapes. Alternatively you could sit in a deckchair or on a papier-mâché rock in front of a painted sea which, luckily for all concerned, would end suddenly where the canvas met the floor. Various more specialised backgrounds served the needs of the military (a stern array of tents) or loving couples (complicated arrangements of stiles or rose-strewn casement windows). Furniture was provided, often ill matched with scenery as changes in backdrops could leave the baronial chair stranded before a turbulent sea. Someone somewhere was doing well out of supplying such furniture, especially after the end of the First World War when there was a sudden vogue which spread from studio to studio for bright, Arts and Craftstyle chairs and benches. The existence of central suppliers is evident from the universal adoption of such trends and the presence of identical ornate stairways and balconies from Portsmouth to Galashiels.

In larger cities more exotic studios flourished which would indulge wilder fantasies in more theatrical situations with appropriate costumes and props. Here gun-toting cowboy could meet Indian squaw or a vamp in top hat and tails could court a gypsy temptress. Pierrots were much in vogue (*fig.7*) and cross-dressing was popular especially in patriotic tableaux involving Britannia and lady soldiers and sailors (*11.i, 11.viii*). For what we would now call a niche clientèle there were bedroom scenes of a mildly risqué sort usually involving two women in pyjamas (stage cigarettes were supplied to add sauciness and sophistication). Backdrops hinted at generic views of the Wild West and the Inscrutable East in a strictly adult world with only rarely a stray child taking part in the fun. The most frequented of such studios in the inter war years was the Fancy Dress Studio in London (at 37 Oxford Street).

You could of course come to regular studios in your own fancy dress, especially if you had contrived something daring or spectacular for a competition or a ball. Customers often supplied their own props, be it a dog or a violin or, in the case of children, a favourite toy or doll. Even a proudly possessed bicycle could be wheeled in front of the scenery.

With the advent of the car and aeroplane some studios (especially at the seaside where air displays were all the rage from 1909) developed a whole new vocabulary of three-dimensional wish fulfilment via sketchy simulations of new travel. This was an advance over the stuffed donkey and the odd beached boat. Rickety aeroplanes (no less rickety in fact than the early craft they imitated) took to the studio skies and cardboard cars sped past painted countryside. Bits of real automobiles were sometimes incorporated and, in the case of motorbikes (*fig.8*) the authentic gleaming machine was waiting for you to set off into (or rather out of, since you had to be seen) the landscape of your choice.

Design of these mock planes and cars roughly kept pace with changes in the originals and the final aeroplane we see before the fashion died away is an impressive fighter-bomber whose gleeful occupants are attacking Berlin (*25.xvi*).

fig.9

One cannot help wondering to what degree the pilots, drivers or passengers of these fictive vehicles found them convincing. None of them would have been in a plane and few even would have travelled in a car: thus they tend to take their imaginary trips rather earnestly. The spirit of fun and irony is largely absent that accompanies comparable cards in which the head is stuck through a hole in a cartoon to make the subject become a bathing belle or an infant in a pram (*fig.9*).

The same question applies to the standard backgrounds where illusion usually ends with remarkable suddenness at the point where the poetic backdrop meets the prosaic floor, a collision often emphasised by a dark gap (*2.viii*). Except in some beach scenes where sand and a clump of seaweed provide continuity there is seldom any attempt to carry through the pastoral or palatial illusion. The odd prop in the form of a deckchair, or potted plant on a stand, is merely placed on the studio linoleum or some crumpled sacking. Perhaps the whole notion of what we now call virtual reality is merely a shifting value, more akin to the theatre's willing suspension of disbelief than any permanent conviction on the part of the viewer. These oddities of enactment never seem to worry the subjects and I have yet to read any message that bothers to mention the issue.

The postcard photographer on his part was even-handed with actuality and illusion. His practice outside the studio left little missing from the catalogue of social existence. The local streets were worked with offers of pictures featuring houses with their occupants, or, more discreetly, portraits taken in the garden or backyard. No wedding, sporting event, religious gathering, pub, shop with staff, boarding-house intake, charabanc outing, fete, parade or amateur dramatic production went unrecorded. Factories and offices were not immune nor those army camps that lacked a resident photographer.

The most remunerative of such concessions was the school visit with its long speciality photo of the whole school for which every parent was, and still is, persuaded to fork out (since somewhere amongst the serried

fig.10

fig.11

scowling and grinning blobs their offspring was to be identified). For the postcard album there were class photographs and pictures of sporting teams and prizewinners. The practice of taking individual portrait photographs of pupils seems only to have got under way in the 1920s. Tinted versions of these head-and-shoulders shots came into fashion and a surprising number of parents opted for tuppence coloured rather than penny plain (*fig.10*).

With their generic flesh tones and appropriate colours for hair and clothing these make up the great majority of surviving tinted cards. Colour film as a popularly available medium did not effectively exist until after the Second World War (*19.vi* is an early example). Though cheapness of labour made hand-tinting only a modest luxury it was not much taken up as an option for the humble postcard. Only about one in a thousand cards that I have seen is tinted. It was not a mechanical process and the results fascinatingly range from the expert gradations achieved by dedicated outworkers to sticky blotches added by amateurs (with the aid of a tinting kit obtained from the local chemist) that often lend a strange expressionist air to otherwise routine scenes and likenesses.

The enforced reliance on monochrome with its repertoire of sepias and rich greenish browns (some of which are merely faded versions of black and white) was an enormous advantage. As one can see from the now universal snaps taken with friendly cameras and fast polychrome film, colour is beyond most people's capacity to handle coherently. Often the most dazzling colour in such a picture belongs to an object we were not interested in when we saw the scene with our differentiating eye. Such unaccountably bright red herrings disperse the narrative when we view what was recorded by the unselective lens.

Our eyes and brains are cleverer than the camera. We look at what is relevant, what we want to know the colour of and to what extent. Paradoxically the brain's response to what the eye takes in is more akin to tinting than it is to colour photography. Black and white pictures have their own colour code: when we watch an old film in the cinema we have no sense of deprivation since the countless gradations between dark and light make up a rich tonal world for our imaginations to interpret and internally tint at will.

It is surprising that there are not more examples of quality tinting, especially in an area like women's fashion, an inexhaustible topic that massively eclipses in variety the dull nuances of change (of course far from dull when really examined) in men's outfitting.

The story of women and their victories of emancipation is by far the era's most stirring tale and a comprehensive parade of shifting styles of dress is one way of telling it. Their political and social liberation is also reflected in fields like education (where interestingly enough the majority of graduation photographs are of women, *fig.11*), transport, sport and employment. The most sudden and significant of these moments of transition is the use in the First World War of women to take over the jobs left vacant by serving men. At the very heart of the home war effort were the munitions factories where women volunteers earned comparable wages to men. For these and other women war workers such as Land Army girls new practicalities of dress added to the prefiguration of inevitable equality.

The Real Photo Postcard not only documents women's progress towards equality but is egalitarian in its own right. Many social barriers fall before it once the lady of the house, the children, the housekeeper, the maid (*fig.12*), the under-gardener and even the dog are all individually content to be pictured in the same style and format. Officers and privates, bosses and members of the workforce, professors and schoolchildren, all hand down records of themselves of the same shape and size and quality. For many a new sense of existential individuality is status in itself and it is a bonus to see themselves on an equal footing. Such an act of levelling set up social reverberations and gave the common and casual seeming postcard a significant role in general social change.

fig.12

Activities were made equal in the same way giving the village cricket team a permanence until then only reserved for famous elevens. The events of a locality (fete, vicar's tea party, Sunday school outing etc.) were as indelibly documented as the grand affairs of the world.

Out of this blanket recording of the nation's life grow the many categories of this ever expanding work. Any account of the psychopathology of collecting will note an attendant need to taxonomise, to establish species and divide them into sub-species. Fission rather than fusion is the dominant process. As numbers build up a heading like *Eating* begins to ramify as indoor and outdoor refreshment are separated, with *Picnics* as a further sub-division.

Out of the 50,000 cards I have collected (themselves whittled down from an inspection of more than two million) some 120 clear categories have emerged as a framework of pigeon holes which would leave few photographs unclassified. Unpredictable groups of cards, such as those where an aspidistra is the common assertive property, grew into piles that demanded autonomy. Having built this schema I was only left with those images where someone was doing or being something but it was not clear what or why. These are filed under the heading *Enigma* (*fig.13*).

As the process became clarified with its unwritten rules (for example, that no picture could hover between categories: it must find its proper home) the goal of the project became more ambitiously unlimited. My initial plan had been to create, so to speak, an alternative National Portrait Gallery, an antidote to the inevitable concentration in the Gallery of certain types and classes of person. If the nation was the sum of all its parts this specific time in history offered the first possibility of truly representing it. It had never before been the case that almost everyone as if in a visual census was accounted for in portrait terms. Needless to say I did not mean to oust the worthy from their frames but at least give, via this transforming period of demotic portraiture, pictorial enfranchisement to those who constituted

fig.13

the nation, bore its children, did its jobs, fought its battles and made it work: to celebrate, in short, the hitherto unsung.

The artist is a curious creature to give himself such a task since he is condemned to make everything he does contribute towards a work of art. Thus as well as this direct goal a larger, hazier enterprise announced itself, analogous to the splendid failure of Walter Benjamin's *Arcades Project*. Benjamin, to paraphrase his elusive scheme, took the arcades of Paris as a structuralist unit through which he could illuminate the world's desires, behaviour, aspirations, artistry and folly, implying that there was nothing that could not be demonstrated or explained through this microcosm and its denizens. With these more manageable postcards I think I am on firmer ground than Benjamin for in them the world is not only unconsciously but consciously, sometimes wilfully, showing itself (and discovering itself). I shall soon escape from this paragraph which begins to be dangerously vainglorious, but not before making the further comparison with aspects of that great poem by Wittgenstein which hides behind the dauntingly academic title *Tractatus Logico-Philosophicus*. One of the themes of the *Tractatus* is that whole areas of describing the world lie outside verbal discourse. They cannot be trapped in the cage of language but can only be shown. Thus whatever this introduction, and the more learnedly analytical essay by Elizabeth Edwards, may discuss, the mysterious quantity that can be shown in this project is infinitely larger than what can be said.

Wittgenstein and Benjamin would each be quite at home with these images not only because they lived and worked through this same period but also because the ludic spirit that lurks behind their high seriousness would have led them on their own eccentric and illuminating paths through

fig.14

such material. Both would have seen that, categories aside, there is at the heart of the project the fundamental human image merely presenting its case. Even a postcard of no one special doing nothing in particular in an unspecified place at a time not readily identifiable and portrayed by an anonymous photographer fills the eye with its eloquence.

Anonymity is of course the order of the day since most cards are uninscribed giving no hint of who the subjects are, nor indication of which photographer took them and where. Sometimes the name of a chain of studios is printed on the back or that of a nationwide firm like Van Ralty or Jerome. Occasionally a handwritten name or two, as in the case of 'Hilda & Walter' inscribed on the back of a card of two Salvationists, *fig.15*, gives a corroborative flavour to the image (as if to say, yes, these are exactly the right names). It is naturally intriguing for me to know that the picture of my mother was taken in London by The Wykeham Studios Ltd of 67 Balham High Road and furthermore that their premises is now Atlas DIY under the directorship of Dr Memon but this does not add much to the project as a whole. Thus except for date, place and photographer, where I have known these details with some certainty (they are given verbatim as they appear on the cards themselves), there are no captions.

This wilful poverty of captioning is ably assisted by my ignorance. I could almost wish I knew even less than I do, for patchy knowledge is seldom helpful. I can recognise, say, the badges of a couple of the more obvious army regiments but I know that there are several people who from a glimpse of half a brass button can identify brigade and rank and date and details of service. Similarly there are experts who can name the make of a car from a partial view of its rear, explaining that a particular exhaust pipe was exclusive to the 1929 Wolseley Cabriolet. Without a whole panel of specialists on costume, engines, spectacles and sporting paraphernalia it is better for me not to rely on guesswork especially since a year ago I lost my nerve while sorting through a pile of cards sent on approval by the reliable Mr Musgrove. Just as I was putting a fine postcard portrait of a nurse in the appropriate file I turned it over only to read the pencilled inscription, 'Aunt Ellen dressed as a nurse for the pageant.' There was a moment of Borgesian bafflement as I suddenly imagined that all these butchers, postmen, sailors and headmistresses were players in a huge carnival of scrambled identities. The panic passed as I put it in the section marked *Make Believe: Adults*, but I was never to know absolute certainty again.

Long before that lesson I had abandoned dating cards by costume since where photographs bear actual dates the clothes do not always tally with those in books on the history of fashion. My guesses could be ten years out. In the case of male attire I only had to remember my father's pride in 1955 over the durability of a suit made twenty years earlier and a tweed overcoat that had served a decade more than that.

Thus with spare or non-existent captions I pass on the advantage of a

fig.15

low level of information and a high degree of the existential authenticity that led me to immerse myself in these images in the first place.

The range of characters and contexts dealt with is nonetheless as complete as the photographic card generously allows, though it should be pointed out that the postcard market, a small but obsessive world that forgathers in dull hotels and bleak municipal halls up and down the country, has, like any other market, its own forces that swell the prices of the sought against the disregarded. Thus certain topics are, because of expense, difficult to collect. Trams, traction engines, railway stations and gypsies have their driven buyers and you would not expect to meet in this book a passenger waving from the rail of the departing Titanic.

Luckily these Real Photo Postcards, especially those which would have come from family albums, are not the prime quarry of collectors. Perhaps their often uncomfortable directness and unequivocal reality still bar the door against nostalgia. If this project had a coat of arms *Forget Nostalgia* would be its motto. Although nostalgia would seem to be a link between us and times gone by it actually builds a barrier that divides us from the past and prevents us engaging with it. All these are pictures of the present; often, in the brevity of youth or the uncertainty of war, urgently so. They themselves commend newness and offer it to the future. This car, this dress, this toy, this office, this uniform are in the world of actuality. This team is this year's eleven, these are my present workmates, this my bride or this my newborn child: all speak of a now that as yet knows no then. It is a misunderstanding to visit quaintness upon them. Fortunately for me most of them end up at the side of dealers' stands in that last stop before the oblivion of unsaleability, the 25p box.

fig.16

By the time I get to a postcard fair the truly dedicated have departed with their spoils. Dogs and fire engines have vanished together with any trace of cards under the headings of Jewish Interest or Hop-Picking. Therefore any apparent bias here against dentistry or fairground scenes is not my own. Shop fronts are enthusiastically collected by local collectors if they can be identified as to their whereabouts, leaving me contentedly with the anonymous and unplaceable residue. Anyone however who wishes to start a collection of cards depicting Anglican clergymen (though some of these too will find a place in our project) can have a field day.

I am happy enough at such markets and gatherings with what in terms of collecting are the remains of the day and, in terms of the scope of this work, the remains of that half century within which a whole nation seemed to stand forward as a visual collective as if to declare with their blended individualities We Are The People.

Little Theatres of Self
Thinking about the Social
Elizabeth Edwards

'I SHALL never forget the day I had that [photograph] taken. I was nine-teen. I was so excited. I practised for days in front of the mirror how I would stand.'[1]

There is something compelling about these modest postcard portraits, their gentle hopefulness within the ordinary – to be someone and to belong somewhere. Yet they are mysteries, for we know little of their sitters or their circumstances. They are orphans, severed from the direct contexts of per-sonal meaning for which they were intended. Faced with this mass of anonymous images we are inevitably frustrated that we cannot know their histories, their individual experiences. We can only weave our own stories around them, not theirs.

So what kind of documents are these? What can we learn from them? Does their anonymity condemn them to the status of trivial curiosity? They are rich in forensic detail (how hair was tied, how boots were buttoned, how bathing costumes sagged), but despite their appearance of evidential plenti-tude there is nonetheless a sense that they are resistant. They promise so much, yet we are left with the feeling that we don't really know, that we can-not ever get beneath the surface of the brightly polished shoes, the carefully arranged lace collar, and the fleeting gesture caught in the moment of photo-graphic exposure. Is it possible to excavate at greater depth?

If they resist the individual, the photographs collectively provide us with a sense of the wider communal world view from which they arose, a world view that made them thinkable in certain forms in the first place. The meanings of portraits are never confined to the personal but are shaped by public and shared needs, shared conventions and shared understandings. It is from this perspective that we can approach this critical mass of postcard portraits. We can attempt to extrapolate the places where community and the desire to belong overlap with the individual and the personal, since, as Pat Holland puts it, 'the personal histories they record belong to narratives on a wider scale, those public narratives of community, religion, ethnicity and nation which make private identities possible'.[2] The repertoire of photographic styles and subjects includes a vast and composite array of per-sons, objects, places and occurrences, the patterns and regularities of which meld them into a rich chronicle of ordinary experience. As such the postcard portraits might be seen as group self-portraits reflecting attitudes, beliefs and assumptions.

There has been extensive work on the photograph as portrait, embrac-ing Marxist, feminist or psychoanalytical approaches, to name just some.[3] Likewise there has been much work on family photography, its idealisations, suppressions and myth-making.[4] While all of these approaches have a bear-ing on this discussion, I am concentrating on how we might approach these photographs, not necessarily in terms of personal memory and experience, but in the broader realms of social history, anthropology and visual culture.[5] My starting point will be a series of 'anthropological' questions, which will perhaps lead us back, closer to the individual. How do these postcard portraits function as social images and social objects, saturated with a culturally specific consciousness? In what ways are they part of the reproduction and performance of social values? What meaning did they have for people? Consequently how do they fit into the social practices of desiring, making and using images, and the ways in which private fantasy interweaves with public history? Out of this, I hope, will emerge an appreciation of the historical density of these unassuming images, how they reveal not a single truth about a person or an age but work as powerful, and perhaps inexhaustible, starting points for the multiple realities from which people constructed their worlds.

THE POSTCARD PORTRAIT

What links all the photographs in this book is their format. They are real photographs, that is, produced by a true photographic process rather than photomechanically, and printed on card measuring approximately $5\frac{1}{2}$ x $3\frac{1}{2}$" (140 x 88mm), the back of which was printed in the still familiar postcard manner.

The picture postcard format was standardised in 1899, and became a very common form in which people received and consumed their photographic imagery in the first quarter of the twentieth century. It had first appeared in the United States but evolved rapidly in Britain from the mid-1890s, when the postal authorities allowed this quick, cheap and convenient form of communication. Initially only the address could be written on the reverse, while a short message was permitted on the front of the card. In 1902 the familiar divided back was established in Britain, the result of changes in postal regulations after which the message could be written on the back.

The postcard portrait flourished from about 1900 to 1935, the major period of production and use being *circa* 1900–1918.[6] Until the advent of photography, owning a likeness of oneself or one's family and friends was the privilege of the wealthy. By the mid-nineteenth century photographic

fig.17

practices of almost industrial scale had developed. *Cartes de visite*, small (2$\frac{1}{8}$ x 3$\frac{1}{2}$", 54 x 88mm) and increasingly cheap mounted photographs, were introduced in 1854, followed in the late 1860s by larger formats such as the cabinet print (6$\frac{1}{2}$ x 4$\frac{1}{4}$", 165 x 108mm). These extended access to photographic portraiture to many more people. While the photographic market tried various formats and gimmicks to replace them, they continued to be used long after they ceased to be fashionable. It was however the advent of the postcard that finally fulfilled both the imaging and social functions of earlier formats. It fast established itself in the market place, becoming one of the main means through which photography and the ownership of some sort of portraiture were placed within financial reach of all but the very poorest.[7]

In some ways the popularity of the postcard for family portraits was enhanced because the format was already well established. They slipped effortlessly into the familiarity of the general mass-market postcard trade of views, celebrities, events, cartoons and kitsch,[8] while at the same time upholding the earlier imaging conventions. They could be collected in specially made albums with pre-cut slots or windows. Thus the portrait postcard taken in the seaside photographer's studio could be juxtaposed with a purchased card of the view of the pier, the promenade, or the sands. This extended the meaning of the portrait by giving people an image of self placed in a narrative of time and space, sometimes reinforced by the identifications in postcards themselves, for instance, 'Seeing Blackpool' (6.*ix*) or Weston-super-Mare (*25.x*).

Although there were major publishers of mass-market postcards, such as Tucks and Valentines, the real photograph portrait postcard was almost exclusively the product of a local photographer's studio, or of itinerant photographers in towns and villages who provided a service for local people in backyards, streets and on beaches. These photographs were developed in the normal way and printed directly onto a piece of card, as glossy or matt prints, the back of which was printed with the conventional postcard rubrics.

fig.18

Photographers' work in this format was not restricted to portraiture. This was simply one of a range of socially important imaging roles undertaken within a local community and reflecting its values – local streets, shops (*26.iii, 26.xi*), the parish church, royal visits, carnivals, pageants (*11.xv, 11.xvii*), accidents, fires and floods.

Such postcard production was also available to the amateur photographer. Postcard format papers were one of a range of choices for printing. Consequently although cards may, in some cases, have been professionally processed, the postcard format itself does not necessarily indicate professional production. This is so especially with the more snapshot-quality, candid photographs of the 1920s and 1930s.[9]

The history of these postcards can also be seen in terms of the democratisation and informalisation of photography. Technological and economic developments steadily placed cheaper and simpler modes of photography within the reach of a growing number of people, giving more opportunities to more people to photograph more moments of everyday life. This process was accompanied by a certain informalisation of social behaviours in front of the camera. Despite the fact that exposure times were already much reduced by the time these portraits were made, the stiff and solemn poses of many of the studio photographs suggest that this was the way people assumed they should present themselves to the camera – this is how photographs were meant to look, perhaps reflecting the importance or rarity of the photographic act (*1.iv, 8.xiv, 13.iii*). Gradually, as photography became more accessible, there are more informal laughing groups of picnickers (*4.i*) or bathers (*36.iii*) or relaxed and unaffected day-trippers in their charabancs (*32.iv, 32.vii, 32.xiv*). Stylistic differences do not necessarily distinguish professional from amateur. The styles interpenetrated one another. The conventions of the studio were reproduced in the backyard (*1.xii*), the groupings of formal portraits were echoed in gardens (*fig.17*), and conversely the levity of the beach infiltrated the studio (*30.v*). In line with broader social changes, we are looking at a shift in the social assessment of appropriateness in relation to photographic behaviours as photography became more familiar and, at the same time, penetrated further into everyday life.[10]

fig.19

LITTLE THEATRES OF SELF

The history of portraiture in general can be related to the parallel history of the concept of identity, and those aspects of identity which are deemed appropriate for portrayal at a given historical moment. Despite its modesty and ubiquity the postcard portrait belongs to a tradition and visual repertoire of imaging the human being, which can be traced back to the emergence of secular portraiture in the fifteenth century.[11] The appropriate forms and intentions that conditioned four centuries of portrait painting, for instance, the Madonna and Child (*17.vi, 17.xvi*), the sober citizen (*10.iii*) or, later, the swagger portrait (*35.xiv*), resonate, as ideal forms, through the postcard portraits.

fig.20

fig.21

fig.22

'The self' is a complex and ambiguous concept, but one that is central to the way we might understand these photographs. There is a massive literature on this subject from psychology, psychiatry, psychoanalysis, sociology and anthropology, which is beyond the scope of this essay. For our purposes I am taking 'the self' to include such defining ideas as autonomy, identity, individuality, liberty, choice and fulfilment. It is through such concepts we understand our passions and desires, display our distinctiveness, model our lifestyles, consume commodities, act out our tastes, fashion our bodies, and so forth. They make us both the kind of persons we really are and shape who we want to be. In other words, it is part of the contemporary apparatus that makes us both human and social.[12] Many of these postcard portraits are, in some way, concerned with the translations from private to public self, expressed through a vernacular aesthetic. All are a form of projection of an ideal, which might be both personal and collective – the happy family, the successful businessman, the brave soldier, the contented worker or simply the lazy, idyllic day on the beach or in the garden. In this they also make visible the abstract norms, values and feelings that surround social life, such as loyalty, respect, attention, happiness, congeniality, trustworthiness, prosperity, solidarity, sobriety and order.

Idealising desires are articulated through the iconographic conventions of the images. They reveal not only certain social expectations of suitable subject matter but also ideas of the correct presentation of self. Ultimately those photographs which give pleasure, and which are accorded the status of 'a good photograph', are those which, through their familiar structure, are able to contain the tension between the longed-for ideal and the ambivalence of lived experience.[13] Wedding photographs, portraits of achievement (*18.xv*), or baby or christening photographs (*fig.18*) must construct and present the protagonists in the right way. This is, of course, most marked in formal studio portraits. However, it is equally present, in a more understated and unconscious way, in the less formal or amateur examples of the genre.

The intensity of these values, as they resonate through specific images, will depend on the intention of the photograph, its role as a public or private statement. This is clear for many images. Some are solemn representations of a ritual self, the formal portrait (*9.v, 27.xxxii*); others are about family relations (*2.xvi,13.v*), or achievement (*18.i*), or memory (*30.xi*). Some are just plain fun (*19.vii, 30.xvi*). Others remain more ambiguous and enigmatic (*14.xix, 15.vi, 26.viii*). While we can only guess at their original intent and meaning through their visual syntax, the portraits nonetheless represent an unarticulated social process through which aspects of community life have become seen as appropriate to photography.[14]

The setting is integral to the performance of the ideal. Studio portraits are the most 'theatrical' in this sense. Here the painted backdrops, decor, furniture and props with which people pose are all intended to be carefully orchestrated for the performance of self. The use of specific props was determined by their social appropriateness. They were sometimes provided by studios to create the solid, worthy and aspirational images which were demanded and reflect the expected social roles – perhaps pretty china for married women, bicycles for adventurous modern young women (*34.iii*), books for both women and men, toys for children (*fig.19*). There is no way of telling if the china, teddy bears or bicycles that feature in so many of these images were owned by the subject of the photograph. Probably many were not, but they all carry a similar social message and simultaneously indicate appropriate moral values. Indeed such is the tenacity of the values attached to objects that many made the transition from the studio to the backyard, garden or even beach, for instance that symbol of elegant domesticity, the potted aspidistra (*1.xi, 1.xii*).

Pose is equally potent. Many photographs, whether studio or amateur, might be seen as 'an act of celebratory co-operation'.[15] The poses refer back to well established representational conventions, often of social superiors, for instance, the sober young cleric photographed with a book against a painted studio backdrop (*21.vii*). Women's portraits, especially of those more self-assured in front of the camera (*fig.20*), perhaps draw their style from fashion magazines or from the aristocratic and elegant images of society photographers such as Bassano Ltd (*19.iv, 31.v*). By the late nineteenth century cheap photomechanical half-tone printing technologies were well established and such imagery was widely disseminated through newspapers and, especially, illustrated magazines, establishing an idea of portraiture in the popular imagination, models for the aspirational self. The glamorous images of actresses and early film stars were emulated in a million postcard portraits of young women (*9.xii*) (*fig.21*).

For many of the subjects of these portraits, photography was probably a rare experience, at least until the First World War. It was the moment when the mythic and the idealised self, in 'Sunday best', was performed. This is so not only of studio photographs, but also of formal photographs taken in quasi-studio conditions such as arrangements in the backyard, perhaps by a

fig.23

fig.24

fig.25

visiting photographer (*fig.23*). Sometimes a new self was portrayed, the photograph marking life changes, for instance the romantically posed munitions worker with a shell case (*22.i*), the young soldier in a new uniform (*35.v*), or the new mother (*17.ii*). Children learned the conventions and traditions of photography, what it meant to have one's photograph taken, through experience of the studio (*fig.22*). For many the seriousness of the photographic experience dominates those occasions that might have allowed greater levity, as demonstrated by the solemnity that pervades holiday or wedding photographs (*2.iv*, *25.xi*).

Group photographs are especially complex. In these we see the play of the individual against the collective, indeed their subject is the performance of the cohesive group. However, these are never neutral but act out hierarchies of gender, age and sometimes class (*figs 24, 25*),[17] for instance, the daughter standing behind elderly parents. One can sometimes sense a tension between the individuals in the group and the social relationships inscribed in the image (*fig.26*). Such portraits are about a whole range of social networks displayed, where what is left out of a photograph is as crucial as what is included. Unhappy marriage, the over-disciplining father and bitter sibling must sometimes exist beneath the social veneer of these seemingly unruffled lives.

For all this careful performance, it is possible to glimpse behind the social façade to the reality of people's experience. The mechanical nature of photography records indiscriminately. It has a random inclusiveness that can destabilise its intended message. Often it is the small unconsidered details which do this.[18] They create points of fracture in the performance, allowing other possible readings of the photograph to emerge – for instance the large workman's hands which protrude stiffly from a smart suit (*13.xvi*, *13.xxi*), the worn toes on the shoes of a carefully groomed child (*fig.27*), the bride and groom standing on a little mat in the street (*fig.28*) or the pale body and weather-beaten face of an outdoor worker on holiday (*36.xvii*). Such details speak volumes, pointing beyond the frame of the photograph to experience hidden beneath the little theatre of self.

It must be remembered that the production of such postcards was not a calculated aesthetic force but a cheap, easy and commercially expedient way of fulfilling the imaging desires of a mass market. The livelihood of these photographic practitioners depended not on innovation, but precisely the opposite: on their ability to produce images which accorded with the conventional expression of specific social desires, whether a christening portrait or fun at the seaside. Even in a period of cheap mass photography, we still turn to the professional photographer to produce the appropriate icon of marriage or graduation. Indeed there is a sense in which the photographer is a kind of shamanistic figure, holding ritual knowledge as to the correct forms through which to express a given social experience, translating people into another realm through his intervention. Anyone who has watched a photographer arranging groups for formal photographs at a wedding can be in no doubt of this.

Many postcard portraits record such special events, the non-ordinary, which mark the flow of life: births, the ceremonies of childhood such as starting school or taking part in a pageant (*3.xxiii*), holidays, outings, special parties or significant birthdays. While each of these carried an expectation and conventional mode of presentation, they were moments marked in themselves. They were defined as 'photographable' in that making a photographic record was an integral part of the event itself. Viewed broadly, it is these occasions, whether getting married or going to war, that connect ordinary lives to traditional social and cultural values and thus to a wider world, transforming and spreading them.[19] Hence their social significance.

There was, as I have suggested, a strong moral dimension to these representations of self – of patriotism, duty, sobriety, order and cleanliness. They were not merely about 'looking your best' or presenting a 'social front' for the photograph, but about a convincing ideal performance of a whole series of associative values. We are being asked to believe not simply in the 'reality' of the photograph but more importantly to believe in the 'truth' of the representational power and significance of the created icon.[20]

fig.26

The photographs also reveal the social processes that affirm values: the ways by which girls are turned into women (*33.xvi*) and boys into men (*figs 29, 30*). Boys are sometimes posed in a way suggesting activity, with a fishing net or a ball, whereas girls' props, perhaps a doll or a posy of flowers (*33.vii*), suggest a more static lifestyle, reflecting the expected gender roles (*fig.31*). The photographs also point to the way in which people learn to be responsible, obedient and dutiful members of society – domestic, civic and imperial – through the transmission of social knowledge (*3.viii, 3.xii, 11.vii, 21.viii, 23.vi, 24.viii, 24.xi*).

Nonetheless, despite the conventional iconography, the postcards also indicate social and political change and many are relentlessly modern, playing with and domesticating air travel (*25.ii, 25.v*), motor cars (*6.ii*) and even war (*25.xvi*). As Tom Phillips points out in his introduction, they are especially revealing in relation to the status of women. On the one hand there are photographs of, one can conjecture, the harassed mother with too many children and too little money (see *fig. 22*). Others suggest the shifting demographic of women in the work place (*8.x, 8.xxiii, 10.xi, 22.iii*). On the other hand there are modern young women with bicycles (*34.ii, 34.iii*), playing tennis (*27.iii*), or taking on men's roles (*11.viii, 22.xv*). Some, especially from the First World War, actually perform for the camera as if they were men in androgynous uniform and adopt a male stance (*22.xii, 22.xiv*). Like the young men in new uniforms, symbolic of their revised identities (*35.v, 35.xxvii*), the women are, very literally, playing their new roles.

These little theatres of self are accentuated by the nature of photography itself, which condenses fragments of time and space within the image frame. This characteristic endows photographs with a peculiar concentration and intensity. The subject matter, that still moment inscribed on the photographic negative, is literally projected forward to the viewer through

fig.27

fig.28

the intense energy confined within it. Through this focus of attention, the most ordinary occurrence, such as standing outside the front door (*5.ix*, *5.xi*) or sitting in the garden, is transfigured into something memorable, the most humble person elevated into 'someone'.

Many of the people, however posed, have a vitality and energetic engagement with the act of being photographed. The sitters present themselves specifically to be seen, to communicate with vibrancy and believability, almost as if we might engage them in conversation (*fig.32*). They have a quiet dignity, a self-possession, a wry amusement. In some cases it is almost as if the subject is too big for the space of the frame, giving a sense of being about to move beyond it towards us (*18.xiv*). What is especially striking about these portraits of ordinary people is that they seem suffused with hope, possibly in some cases against all the odds. We cannot know.

SOCIAL OBJECTS

The social desires and values that envelop individual postcards – love, friendship, community, well being, and remembrance – are entangled with broader social functions. Photographs mediate between peoples within communities. They are stories that those communities are telling about themselves – who they are and their relationship to others.

The term 'communities' here is not restricted to the usual sense of a village or a street, but includes kin groups, age groups, class groups or interest groups. These different and overlapping groups, which make up people's identities within the community, are held together through systems of exchange. These involve not only objects but also common meanings and understandings. We have seen how postcard portraits work to communicate social values. They can thus be seen as part of the rhetoric that holds communities together, making values concrete as active intermediaries in social networks.

Consequently, these postcards are not simply images but objects with a social function. The whole idea of postcards was that they were message-carrying objects. As such they are enmeshed in a whole series of cultural behaviours related to swapping, gifting, keeping, displaying and viewing. Indeed the destruction of photographs, burning that of an ex-husband or wife, for instance, is often related precisely to a rupture in social relations. Some postcards carry direct messages within them, such as OKRU or OU2 marked on fantasy aircraft (*25.xii*, *25.xiii*). They may be jokes but they point to a serious social function.

Which photographs were kept and which were not is based not necessarily on the historical accuracy of an image but on a standard of meaning that the image upheld.[21] As objects we can conjecture that the postcards were given and received with pleasure, the exchange cohering a relationship. Few of these portrait postcards have actually been sent in the conventional way, through the post. They appear either to have not been sent at all or to have been enclosed within an envelope, messages covering the whole of the back including the address space. Used in the home, they were perhaps displayed, formally framed in its semi-public spaces, or in more private spaces, such as bedrooms or dressing rooms. Others were hidden away in boxes, lockets, wallets or family bibles. Others were placed in the narrative of family album, that reliquary of the social. Photographs take their place amongst other things. They are linked perhaps to other objects of special significance, such as souvenirs and gifts, in secular shrines on the chimneypiece or parlour table, becoming public statements of identity and group cohesion.[22] Thus as objects of familial and community communication, the act of owning and cherishing the photograph as a trace of its subject was arguably as important as the image content itself. As a piece of material culture, the postcard portraits, like other photographs, come to stand for relationships. They exist in the spaces between people as well as between people and things, defining who we are within broader social networks.

Many social functions of photographs revolve around memory (*19.xiv*). All these portraits are at one level concerned with the desire to recollect.[23] While family photographs are indeed integrally linked to remembrance, marking and making past experience visible, these photographs cannot be reduced to a nostalgic 'pastness'. For their makers and users they were also about the future, the realisation that the past will play a part in the future. They anticipate the memory of tomorrow, that there will be a need to remember the seaside holiday, the wedding or the first communion. This is not nostalgia, a trivialising romantic sentimentality that removes the past from an active relationship with the present. Rather it is an active embedding of oneself into the flow of social time, recognising the need to tell stories.[24] Even those images demanding an element of pathos, such as the young men in uniform, dated 1914–1918, had the dual function of memory during separation, but the hope of safe return.

fig.29

Photographs imprint themselves on memory and empower narratives of the past, allowing them to be experienced as real or true. All these photographs in their different ways satisfy the need for a story, which haunts each group of people because, ultimately, stories are not told by photographs but by the different readings brought to them. Their signs, despite the best efforts of their makers and sitters, are endlessly recodable. In their social function, the photographs are not merely objects of the silent contemplation of individual memory. They are linked to the clamour of oral testimony, engaging not just sight but sound and even smell. Spoken histories are told with and around photographs, as people weave their stories looking at albums or passing round the photographs from the old shoebox under the bed – 'we did have fun in Weston super Mare' (*25.x*).

CONCLUSION

Postcard portraits such as these can, as Jo Spence puts it, 'operate at … [the] junction between personal memory and social history, between public myth and personal unconsciousness'.[25] From them we can extrapolate a wealth of

fig.30

fig.31

fig.32

social detail, from the material culture of everyday life to social change. Using the images to think with, however, we can delve much deeper into how people negotiated their place in the world, what they thought they were, what they hoped to be. The photographs are saturated with the hopes and secret fears of ordinary people, making statements about themselves, desiring to be remembered – to be someone if only for a moment. This is important because it is too easy to read these images simply with an undifferentiated and reductionist nostalgia. The latter obscures not only the ambiguities and tensions within images such as these, but loses sight of the specifics of cultural experience that made them possible. In the anthropological view one cannot exist without the other.

In some ways it is difficult to say anything about the postcard portraits – because they say everything. They connect to almost every aspect of experience. Their importance as a social document is that they constitute a self-generated history, however fragmented it might be. It is a voice that is seldom heard in the official histories, yet it is entangled with the great movements of 'History' – war, social change, and economic depression. Photographs operate on a very different historical register from other sources. The postcard portrait has its own particular and pertinent place, being directly concerned with a people's 'voice' about themselves, for themselves. An anthropological approach to these ephemeral fragments of popular experience – looking at the patterns and processes of the whole, an understanding grounded on the careful excavation of the specific practices – goes some way to reclaiming their power and meaning. We might still not be able to put names to the faces, but we can move towards constructing the social world in which these postcards had meaning for people, and as such perhaps give them an empowering voice in the present.

NOTES

1. Unnamed female informant quoted in Jeremy Seabrook, 'My life is in that box' in Holland and Spence, *Family Snaps*.
2. Holland, Introduction, *Family Snaps*, pp.1–2.
3. For instance Brilliant, *Portraiture*; Clarke, *The Portrait in Photography*; Woodall, *Portraiture: Facing the Subject*.
4. *See* Hirsch, *Family Photographs: Content, Meaning and Effect*; Hirsch, *Family Frames: Photography, Narrative and Postmemory*; Langford, *Suspended Conversations*; Holland and Spence, *Family Snaps*.
5. There is a massive literature on 'people's history' or 'history from below', for instance the agenda laid down by Raphael Samuel in the now classic volume *People's History and Socialist Theory* and the work of the History Workshop. One of the features of this movement has been the shift towards the study of the subjective experience of ordinary people.
6. In 1904 in Britain alone more than seven million postcards were sent through the post. If one includes portrait postcards, which were often sent within letters, the figure must have been very considerably larger.
7. Many factories had Photograph Clubs. Workers paid a few pence per week and a lottery or rota system decided who visited the photographic studio, thus spreading the cost of owning a photograph for the very poor. Photographic Clubs often had special arrangements with local studios. It is likely that some of the portraits in this book result from such arrangements. *See* Linkman and Warhurst, *Family Albums*, p.24.
8. *See* Phillips, *The Postcard Century*, for examples.
9. Phillips, *The Postcard Century*; Willoughby, *A History of Postcards*.
10. Boerdam and Martinius, 'Family Photographs – a sociological approach' in *Netherlands Journal of Sociology*, pp.108.
11. *See* Hirsch, *Family Photographs*, pp.15–46.
12. This definition comes from Rose, *Inventing Ourselves*, pp.1–2.
13. Holland, *Family Snaps*, p.4.
14. Boerdam and Martinius, 'Family Photographs', p.99.
15. Holland, *Family Snaps*, p.4.
16. For poor working-class boys the First World War offered a new sense of belonging, a newly discovered or assumed personal identity. In some cases, these photographs were taken in photographers' studios that were set up in and around the camp. T. and V. Holt, *Till the Boys Come Home*, p.32.
17. *See* Philip Stokes, 'The Family Photograph Album: So Great a Cloud of Witness' in Clarke, *The Portrait in Photography*, pp.196–7.
18. Roland Barthes described this as 'punctum' – that tiny point of random inscription within the photographs that disrupts the social surface – in *Camera Lucida*.
19. Hirsch, *Family Photographs*, pp.40–42.
20. For an extended discussion of these ideas *see* Goffmann's now classic book *The Presentation of Self in Everyday Life*. See also Pols, *Family Photographs 1860–1945*, p.61.
21. Hirsch, *Family Photographs*, p.12.
22. For the social use of photographic objects *see* for instance Bourdieu, *Photography: A Middle Brow Art*, pp.31–9; Edwards and Hart, *Photographs Objects Histories*; Freund, *Photography and Society*.
23. An enormous amount has been written on the relationship between photography, memory and death. For instance Barthes, *Camera Lucida*; Hirsch, *Family Frames*; Langford, *Suspended Conversations* etc and references therein.
24. In many working-class households photographs are the only surviving documents of family history. Linkman and Warhurst, *Family Albums*, p.2.
25. Spence, *Family Snaps*, pp.13–14.

Postcards

Aspidistra

1.i

To start this book with such an apparently marginal topic might seem perverse, yet the aspidistra has for me become somehow emblematic of the whole project. It emerges as a subject from the mass of cards by its insistent presence in so many circumstances. It is a sign by which you know you are in the true postcard world.

The aspidistra was in fact such a staple of domesticity that it was immortalised in a song made famous by Gracie Fields, 'The Biggest Aspidistra in the World'.

It can indeed be an elegant plant as in *1.ii* where it rhymes with the pose and drapery of an elegant woman. It can also have a melancholy air as in *1.v* when its leaves turn down. Its popularity derives from its fabled resilience. As another artistic celebrant of the 'parlour palm', George Orwell, points out it requires quite an effort of neglect to kill an aspidistra off, though the four females in *1.xiii* seem to have managed.

There are enigmas. It is no mystery that when the child moves in *1.x* the aspidistra stays still, but more sinister when the lady and dog in *1.xi* stay still and the plant decides to stretch its leaves. In *1.xiv* it has a predatory air and its seated companion looks uneasy, while in *1.xix* a more subtly unusual appearance of an aspidistra occurs, where it seems to have wandered into the countryside to take up its traditional photographic position.

1.ii

1.iii

1.iv

1.v W. Cooper, Heckmondwike

1.vi

1.vii

1.viii

1.ix

1.x

1.xi Sheffield

1.xii Portland

1.xiii

1.xiv

1.xv

1.xvi Hether & Co., Heathfield

1.xvii Stickybacks, Chatham

1.xviii

1.xix 1930

2.i

Of the backgrounds available at even the most modestly appointed studio a sea scene was one of the most popular. Paradoxically most of these marine portraits were photographed in seaside towns in rooms well within earshot of wave and wheeling gull. Indeed they often included local elements like a pier or Blackpool's big wheel.

The sea is not always calm in the photographer's studio, for agitated waves make a more exciting picture. Various degrees of verisimilitude are attempted with sand heaped up and papier-mâché rocks strategically placed. But just as often the sea ends abruptly as the backdrop reaches the floor and no one seems alarmed or disappointed. Extra drama could if required be supplied, at least in Yarmouth,

by the offer of oilskins. This accounts for the heightened atmosphere of *2.x* as opposed to *2.xviii*, which uses the same background. One guesses that *2.xviii* was taken by an assistant on the photographer's day off: having the pier emerge from the man's ear was not a recommended compositional device.

There is one other duplication of a painted cloth in this group, but it takes some looking for. Mood and model often are well matched. What more appropriate background could rise behind the angst ridden man in *2.iv* than this expressionistic ocean, at odds with the rustic seat and colliding with a beach formed of imitation parquet linoleum?

2.ii Walter Bros, Margate

2.iii Valentine's, Folkestone

2.iv Gregson & Co., Blackpool

2.v While U Wait Studios, Blackpool

2.vi 1928 Ramsgate

2.vii Southsea

2.viii

2.ix Ansell, Sandown, I.O.W.

2.x Read's Studios, St. Peter's Road, Yarmouth

2.xi A. Paterson, Leith

2.xii Royal Studio, Weston. S. Mare

2.xiii Anderson, Brighton

2.xiv Southend

2.xv J. H. Seaman, Southport

2.xvi

2.xvii

2.xviii 1928 Read's Studios, St. Peter's Road, Yarmouth

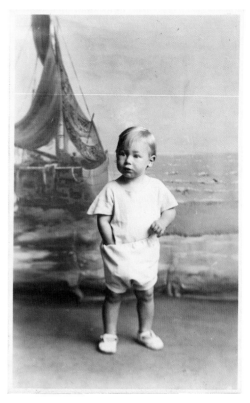

2.xix

2.xx

2.xxi Clocktower Studios, Margate

Make Believe Children

3.i

The products here of the junior department of the school of make believe are largely home grown, some quite elaborately made. The themes by and large replicate those of adults with evergreen favourites like the Gypsy Girl and the Oriental Maiden, or imitate more factual aspects of an adult world just out of reach, such as the knowing nurse (3.x) and the jaded Land Army girl (3.xv). One genre in which the infants score is the cute historical, where miniaturisation is part of the joke. Lilliputian Kaisers and Napoleons pose no threat. But real history is present in the attitudes of all these images whether theatrical, military, ethnic or sociological. The golliwog may now have passed through and out the other side of controversy and perhaps we would now find more disturbing echoes in 3.viii, which shows a boy dressed as an African warrior. The slippers are a mistake but the rest is convincing enough, unsurprisingly since the shield and the spear are authentic. They were no doubt brought back by the father who had acquired them in circumstances best left unguessed at. As in the postcard the Union Jack is not far away.

The picture above is the most enigmatic. What pastoral episode is being enacted we cannot tell but (despite the hint of everyday clothes) it captures the lost magic of that Arcadian world that never was. For those that think the power of advertising is new 3.xxvi and 3.xxvii quote well known advertisements of the period; 3.xxvi promotes Skippers Sardines and 3.xxvii of course mimics the Millais painting *Bubbles*, which advertises Pears Soap.

3.ii

3.iii

3.iv

3.v

3.vi

3.vii E. Simmons, Herne Bay

3.viii Wembley

3.ix

3.x Raie Studios, Hammersmith

3.xi Herbert, Lancaster

3.xii Fancy Dress Studio, London

3.xiii Leek, Staffs

3.*xiv* Dura Ltd

3.*xv*

3.*xvi* Palmer, Tower Studios, Herne Bay

3.*xvii*

3.xviii

3.xix

3.xx Van Ralty Studios

3.xxi

3.xxii A. Hunter, Manchester

3.xxiii

3.xxiv W. A. Brown & Son, Manchester

3.xxv Gale's Studios

3.xxvi 1932 Waltur Studios, Walthamstow

3.xxvii

Picnic

4.i

The postcard picnic is windless and midge-free and does not induce sore elbows. If more pleasure is sometimes communicated than was actually had, it is still by and large a cheerful theme.

The picnic is the province of the amateur with a camera, but the success rate is high thanks to generous daylight and the natural way in which people group themselves. With so many props and tasks everyone has something to do, even if it is only eating.

Though the bicycle picnic had extended the range of locations it was the car with its capacity to carry more ambitious paraphernalia that transformed the family

outing whose highlight was always an alfresco meal.

The English need for tea brought an elaboration to arrangements and few of our picnickers are lacking the necessaries of kettle, teapot and crockery. Even though the sophisticated ladies in 4.vi have a flask they still maintain the proprieties by using proper cups and saucers.

In all these cards one has to give a thought (unless technical trickery has been employed) to the missing picnicker. In 4.vii what seems a tête-à-tête idyll is actually lacking its photographer. In 4.ix the man with the camera would balance the sexes and make sense of the whole adventure.

4.ii

4.iii

4.iv

4.v

4.vi

4.vii 1906 Brighton

4.viii

4.ix

4.x Paignton

4.xi

House the Terrace

5.i

Long streets and terraces of undetached houses are at the heart of urban Britain's vigorous monotony: though not involving much in the way of architectural invention they employ all kinds of ornamental devices cribbed from more exalted buildings.

Such houses form one of the most common real-life backdrops for the postcard and allow their owners or occupants to speak of property, position and pride. Many of these familiar buildings were relatively new when photographed and are seen with their original ironwork railings, stripped in the two world wars to supply munitions factories. The itinerant street photographer went from house to house in working hours. Thus it is usually the woman, or women, of the house that we see.

Such a house-to-house survey would be impossible today since cars now line every street as I have found when doing '20 Sites n Years' (an annual photographic project of urban record that I started in 1973). This factor may have led to the relatively early fall from fashion of such a postcard genre. You may think that your house has never been the subject of a postcard and that there exists no postcard photograph of your road. You are probably wrong on the first count and almost certainly on the second. The local enthusiasts for topographic cards are likely to have both in their collections.

5.ii

5.iii

5.iv

5.v

5.vi

5.vii

5.viii

5.ix

5.x

5.xi

5.xii

5.xiii

5.xiv

5.xv

Fantasy Transport by Car

6.i Weston. S. Mare

The transport offered to those for whom motoring was only a dream ranged from the simplest cut-outs to the machines themselves, stranded in a studio or beached on the sands. Various backgrounds urban or pastoral (or even exotic as in *6.xiv*) were offered, sometimes in association with the same vehicle.

The postcard photo haltingly followed advances in car design right up to the racy 1930s. The heyday however of motoring wish-fulfilment was in the period before the First World War when the design of cars approached a standardised form. Most of these willing and often solemn

passengers would never actually have been in a real motorcar. True motoring dress was ignored though we see it mimicked in *6.ii* where a charade-like simulation of a car has been wittily assembled in someone's backyard: everyone is correctly wrapped up, the driver has his goggles on and the women have their hats properly tied down.

The trio above seem to be having the most fun. The boy has claimed the coveted privilege of steering. With a contented passenger on the right and the radiant woman in the middle they are setting off from their baronial estate in high style.

6.ii 1911

6.iii

6.iv Morecambe

6.v While U Wait Studios, Blackpool

6.vi

6.vii

6.viii

6.ix Electric Studios, Blackpool

6.x

6.xi Hamptons, Glasgow

6.xii

6.*xiii* Mr B's Studio, Glasgow

6.*xiv* Electric Studios, Blackpool

Dance

7.i
J. W. Debenham

Most postcards of dancers or dancing feature small girls. Even a few ballet classes would seem to qualify a child for portrayal in the style of the then current cards of celebrity ballerinas.

Whereas (mercifully) the image of the aspiring violinist makes no give-away squawks, the picture of the apprentice dancer tells all. One knows with immediate certainty that 7.iv and 7.v will never be seen at Covent Garden whereas 7.ii, and especially 7.iii, have (at least to the untrained eye) a bodily poise and focus that might be worth encouraging.

Occasionally one spots in a group of infant dancers the real thing. The little barefoot girl in 7.xxii (far left) with her head inclined epitomises that moment (and it may have been merely transient) when the dancer becomes the dance and is transfigured by her dancing. As in the theatre atmospheric lighting (here courtesy of the sun) is a great help.

When it comes to adults the whole effect can be more embarrassing. The excuse of childhood has gone and gracelessness allied to pretension can be irremediably mawkish. Isadora Duncan and the proponents of free dance have a lot to answer for in the tableau above. The men at their ballroom dancing in 7.xi come as a somewhat enigmatic relief.

It is easy, as I demonstrate, to be lured into judgement but that has nothing to do with the project. All these dancers are in a true sense completely authentic and one's temptation to allot points to the three girls doing the splits is a pleasant but quite secondary game.

7.ii Ideal Studios, Perth

7.iii T. A. Mann, Hastings

7.iv De Freyne Studios, Mansfield

7.v

7.vi

7.vii

7.viii

7.ix

7.x

7.xi Barrett's Photographers, London

7.xii Jerome Ltd

7.*xiii*

7.*xiv* The Fancy Dress Studio, London

7.*xv* Boydes Studios, London

7.*xvi* 1934 J. E. Bradley

7.xvii H. W. Winter, Derby

7.xviii Walter Biggs, Bristol

7.xix Dorondo Mills' Studios, Liverpool

7.xx

7.xxi

7.xxii

7.xxiii Gale's Studios

7.xxiv De Freyne Studios, Mansfield

7.xxv

Workers the Factory

8.i

There is no equivocation in the world of machines and art has long been jealous of their perfect marriage of form and function. Machinery as an ensemble has its own poetry of orchestrated shapes like the repeated wheels in *8.xxi*, each of which has a structure long ago predicted in the art of ornament.

Those of us who do not work in such an arduous and often dangerous environment are free to indulge ourselves in the aesthetics of the matter, yet it is evident from these images that both workers and the visiting photographer were completely aware of this dynamism.

Pride in the mastery of powerful machines is evident as well as pleasure in the product. Both can be seen in the group of workers and technicians gathered above within the iron flower of a chimney top. Similar satisfaction is shown by the munitions workers in *8.xxiv* at the

beginning of the First World War. Many of them will soon be seeing the other side of such labour when they head for the front and are replaced by women volunteers (see Women in Uniform, p.199).

In pictures of women millworkers there is a shift of emphasis towards the human. The camaraderie of toil is the aspect most frequently demonstrated. Women tend not to gain power by their association with the complexity of the machines they work at. Drudgery and long hours are compensated for by lip-read conversation and snatched moments of intimacy.

It is particularly obvious in this section that a constant theme of the cards in this book is modernity and that what is most eagerly shown is the new. I do not know what the installation in *8.xxv* actually does but can sense the excitement as the latest advance in technology is inaugurated.

8.ii

8.iii

8.iv

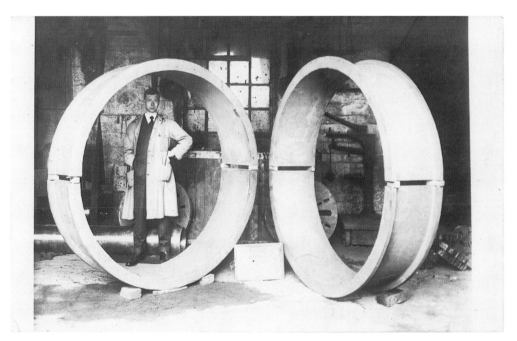

8.v

8.vi

8.vii

8.viii

8.ix Jerome Ltd

8.x 1909

8.xi 1915

8.xii

8.xiii

8.xiv Walk Mill

8.xv Rawtensall

8.xvi

8.xvii

8.xviii

8.xix

8.xx

8.xxi

8.xxii

8.xxiii

8.xxiv

8.xxv

Hair Women

9.i A. Webb, Eastleigh

The great cartwheels of hats that women wore early in the twentieth century called for fortresses of hair to support them. These were built out (with cunning additions) and flattened at the top where the hat rested with the further help of fearsome pins. Without the hat the style has its own winged beauty but it could not outlast the need and desire for less encumbrance. The shift to extreme shortness was radical as, often in the face of parental rage, young women went to get their hair 'bobbed'.

A fair proportion of the women shown here have timed their visit to the portrait studio to follow on from a session at the hairdresser and there are fine examples of hair freshly frizzed or Marcel Waved. Occasionally the more eccentric styles that emerged look as difficult to sustain as the former glories. The slightest fault in either 9.i or 9.xxii would make for scrappy incoherence. No such threat attends the tight crimped styling of 9.xxi whose owner is so pleased she seems to prefer it to her face.

Some styles have an almost sculpted appearance and certainly one cannot imagine the woman in 9.xi running her fingers through her hair, whereas in 9.xiv and 9.xv the triangular style looks particularly vulnerable to scarecrow disarray.

9.*ii*

9.*iii* Rosalind Studios, Stratford on Avon

9.iv

9.v H. M. Veale & Co., Bristol

9.vi

9.vii Mackworth, Peterboro

9.viii The Royal Studios, Blackburn

9.ix 1912

9.x Percy Landon, Watford

9.xi Alfred McCann, Uttoxeter

9.*xii* 1928 Laurence

9.*xiii* Boyd's Studios, Battersea

9.*iv*

9.*xv* Emberson, S.W. London

9.xvi R. L. Knight, Barnstaple

9.xvii Stacey Ward's Studio, Battersea

9.xviii 1927 Stacey Ward's Studio, Battersea

9.xix Jerome Ltd, Manchester

9.xx Miss Potter, Penge

9.xxi

9.xxii 1932

9.xxiii Bradley & Blowers, Colchester

9.*xxiv* 1939

9.*xxv* 1940 Eastbourne Photo Co., Clapham

9.*xxvi* 1938 Jerome Ltd

9.*xxvii* 1939 Leone, Croydon

Workers the Office

10.i 1929

The word 'office' does not conjure up associations of glamour. There is a heroism in manual work and a romantic grandeur in the industrial scene that the office does not quite possess, despite its higher social status. Yet there are offices of spectacular size with Metropolis-like perspectives of desks and modern equipment. These can be contemporary with views of Dickensian toil in worlds that the telephone has scarcely penetrated and where pen and ink and rubber stamp still reign. It is only by degrees that the poetry of office life, as shown here, steals over one. Many are dreams of light and progress, somehow more humanised by the presence of women.

Women rapidly colonised areas of the office where, with no precedent for male domination, innovative techniques were employed. They first infiltrated that arena as typists (or typewriters as they were originally called). Yet the hierarchical pyramid remained constant. Women at their typewriters and dictaphones are important sections of the orchestra, but the soloists and conductors remain male (with the exception of a headmistress in *10.xvi*).

By virtue of calendars, usually present in one form or other, office scenes are often datable to the day.

10.ii 1938

10.iii 1922

10.iv

10.v 1913

10.vi 1912

10.vii

10.viii S. G. Griffith, Haverfordwest

10.ix

10.x

10.xi

10.xii

10.xiii

10.xiv

10.xv

10.xvi

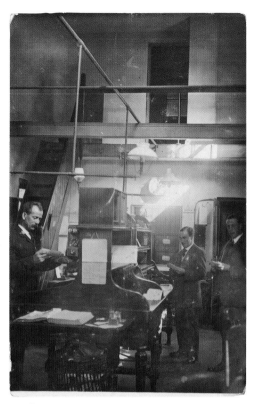

10.xvii

10.xviii

10.xix

10.xx

10.xxi

10.xxii

10.xxiii

10.xxiv

10.xxv

10.xxvi

10.xxvii

Patriotic

11.i

An unembarrassed fervour for king and country was once a component of every fete, parade, gala or even session of home dressing-up. An infinite yardage of Union Jack material seemed to be available. The central figure in all such manifestations is that of Britannia and the girl or woman chosen to represent her (borrowing the Roman pose from the penny coin) inevitably gives a performance as dedicated and solemn as a character in a Passion Play.

During the First World War the flags of Britain's allies are often on show and the various armed forces are represented, frequently with women dressed in the appropriate uniforms. I was born on Empire Day (i.e. 24 May) 1937 which seemed initially to have been a shrewd move. At primary school we dressed in whatever uniforms we were entitled to wear (Cubs, Brownies etc.) and in the bunting-festooned playground had what seemed an extended morning playtime followed by the afternoon off. By the time I left secondary school a sheepish comment on British pluck by the headmaster in assembly was all that remained of the festival spirit.

When was the last sighting of an unironic Britannia? Whatever was the fate of John Bull (*11.vii*)? He was going out of fashion before the Second World War. The cross of St George, asserting tribal rivalry, seems to have ousted both on the terraces.

11.ii Stanley Bros, Leytonstone

11.iii

11.iv Herbert Tear, Clapham

11.v

11.vi J. & G. Taylor, London N.

11.vii Van Ralty

11.viii The Fancy Dress Studio, London

11.ix

11.x

11.xi

11.xii

11.xiii H. Abba, Hull

11.xiv

11.xv

11.xvi

11.xvii

11.xviii

11.xix

11.xx

11.xxi

11.xxii

11.xxiii Fred Wall, Pilsley

11.xxiv J. H. Treloa, Redruth

Pram

12.i

The pram which had ranged from a black tub on wheels to the most elaborate refinement of the coachbuilder's art has more or less disappeared. The pushchair prototypes of the modern streamlined buggy made an early appearance, though perambulator pride with its attendant niceties of fancy pillows and coverlets persisted into the 1960s, even when there was no nurse or nanny to fuss over the carriage or wheel it out.

A look at the wheels of early prams and their primitive shock-absorbing springs shows what boneshakers they must have been; pitching like small boats perched on top of two pennyfarthing bicycles. We have learned too late from experts such as Dr Marvin Sackner that this motion is actually beneficial: indeed it is simulated in his most recent hospital installations for adults. All the more valuably heroic then are the deeds of past pram-pushers like the two families in *12.xii* who have steered two laden prams across pebble and sand to picnic on the beach.

In *12.xiii* we see a man, presumably the grandfather, at least nominally in charge of a pram though the general effect of the image is sinister. Men had a high resistance to pram management which makes *12.xxviii* taken in the 1930s a more radical picture than one might think.

The advent of the fitted car seat has divided child transport management more equally between parents and the answer to whatever happened to the pram is that it disappeared inside the car.

12.ii

12.iii

12.iv

12.v

12.vi Snaps, Bridlington

12.vii

12.viii 1925 East Ham

12.ix

12.x

12.xi Horfield Common

12.xii

12.xiii

12.xiv

12.xv

12.xvi

12.xvii

12.xviii Harold J. Gross, Calne

12.xix

12.xx 1932 Ramsgate

12.xxi

12.xxii

12.xxiii

12.xxiv

12.xxv

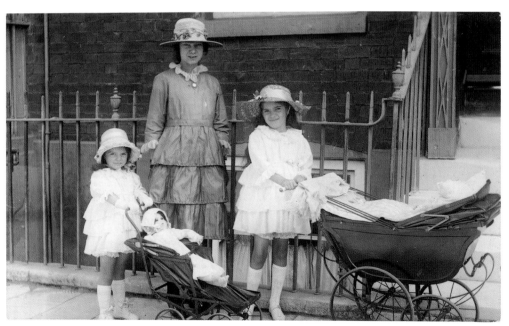

12.xxvi

12.xxvii

12.xxviii

Two Men

13.i The Cosway Studio, Aberdeen

What causes two men to choose to be photographed together? Some such couples can be readily identified as brothers or father and son. The others may be more distant relatives or colleagues or friends, or even lovers, though if that were the case they would have had to be discreet and inconspicuous in their affection. One might hazard a supposition, for example, that the two men in *13.xxii* were treading a high wire in pre-war Tonypandy. Nuances of physical gesture change with the decades and are liable to be misread. Thus the inevitable narratives that build up as one studies almost any of these images might start with inappropriate premises. A case in point is the picture of two fishermen above, on which all kinds of stories could be based and from which a writer like Conrad could conjure a whole novel. All we know is that sometime before the First World War this photograph was taken at the Cosway Studio, Union Street, Aberdeen. Research could yield more information. The different weaves of their jerseys would indicate where among the Scottish islands these were made. It seems that at least one West African fisherman settled in Scotland and took up crofting. Such enquiry, however, has never been a part of this project. In this instance the Holmesian moment would occur when one came to consider the role of the photograph on the table (certainly not an accident), which might play the part of the celebrated dog who did not bark in the night. It was this damaged card bought for 40p that more than any other suggested what resonances the photographic postcard portrait could offer, since every image is poised both at the end and the beginning of a narrative that we cannot know but cannot help speculating about. What gives such a card as this its power is that its subjects know completely who and what they are and where and why.

13.ii Millard & Co., Wigan

13.iii E. Thomas, Imperial Studio, Custom House E.

13.iv

13.v Taylor & Kelf, Great Yarmouth

13.vi G. A. Laver, Thornton Heath

13.vii USA Studios

13.viii Mr Stickyback, Birmingham, Leicester,
Dublin, Glasgow

13.ix 1910

138

13.x

13.xi

13.xii 1937 Sunny Snaps, London

13.xiii

13.xiv Jerome Ltd

13.xv

13.xvi Gale's Studios, Manchester

13.xvii

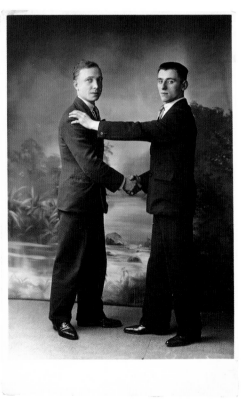

13.xviii

13.xix

13.xx Alf J. Lee, The Palace Studios, Carlisle

13.xxi

13.xxii Crown Studios, 190 Dunraven St., Tonypandy

13.xxiii

13.xxiv Gale's Studios

13.xxv

13.xxvi

Music

14.i

Some of these images would be well worth listening to whereas a few make one grateful for the silence of postcards. It would be a bad day if *14.iv* moved in next door but none of the other string soloists need be feared. In fact I suspect that *14.v*, with his cheerful demeanour plus correct hand positions, might have gone far.

Indeed it is curious how one can intuit the sort of sound being made by these players and groups of players. All parents will instinctively know the noise that the recorders *14.x* make and those who frequent music summer schools will immediately catch an echo in *14.xiii* of some variations on a folk song. Most

would prefer to listen to *14.xiv*, the dapper saxophonist, than to 'Lovely Wales' performed, no doubt with diligence, by *14.xxiv*.

Music can of course be mere mime and *14.xxv* is just sitting at the Butlin's Holiday Camp organ while the mandolin of *14.xxix* is no more than a romantic prop, unlike the two concertinas of *14.xxxvii* with which he performs his party trick.

Most mysterious of all and suggestive of New Age communing with nature is the brass band seen above which looks to be giving a concert to delight the ears of a lake.

14.ii Van Ralty

14.iii Sharnelle, Boscombe

14.iv J. Wilson, Bradford

14.v

14.vi 1929 Gale's Studios

14.vii USA Studios

14.viii Millard & Co., Wigan

14.ix

14.x

14.xi

14.xii 1917

14.xiii

14.xiv

14.xv

14.xvi

14.xvii Ward's & Day Electric Light Studios, Willesden

14.xviii

14.xix

14.xx

14.xxi Walter Scott, Bradford

14.xxii Royal Standard Photo Co., Evesham

14.xxiii

14.xxiv

14.xxv Butlin's Holiday Camp, Skegness

14.xxvi

14.xxvii

14.xxviii

14.xxix

14.xxx

14.xxxi

14.xxxii

14.xxxiii 1937 Sunbeam Photo Ltd, Margate

14.xxxiv

14.xxxv

14.xxxvi

14.xxxvii

14.xxxviii

14.xxxix

People with Animals Dogs

15.i 1924 G. A. Fidler, Stourbridge

I know very little about the various breeds of dog but from the hundreds of postcards I have looked at in which dogs appear it would seem that today's more exotic types were once less common. One sees fewer neotenised miniatures and genetically modified monsters in the first half of the twentieth century. Most seem to be of the kind one might call Spot or Rover.

Dogs are allegedly supposed to look like their owners though I cannot say that the case is proven. The pairings in *15.iv* and *15.v* might qualify however, and the lady and dog in *15.xiii* seem eloquent partners in melancholy.

The nice thing about dogs on postcards is that they do not bark or bite and being myself rather wary of dogs (as they have noticed) I can here enjoy them without a qualm.

In strong contrast to commercially produced cards featuring dogs these images tend not to be sentimental, and even in *15.ii* the charm of the cheerful girl with her mournful dog is spontaneous. The picture above demonstrates the perfect context where the world's most ordinary dog has a special place in both family and composition. This is not the first time that postcard dogs have been on parade. Libby Hall's excellent series *Prince and Other Dogs* sets a high standard in unsentimental appreciation of subject and image.

15.ii 1914

15.iii

15.iv

15.v

15.vi R. Guideminot, Paris

15.vii 1918

15.viii The Palace Studio, Derby

15.ix

15.x G. W. Ash, Walworth Rd

15.xi Herbert Vieler, Imperial Studio, Bexhill

15.xii

15.xiii

15.xiv 1923

15.xv

15.xvi

Children in Uniform Boys

16.*i* Premier Studios, E. Ham

I also was once this serious Cub, solemnly sworn to Be Prepared (not such a bad motto for life as it turned out) and proud of my new uniform for which sacrifices had to be made. I seem to remember a lot of pleading for a particular kind of woggle, the leather ring that fastens the scarf.

Cubs, Scouts and the Boys' Brigade were an important part of schoolboy life in the mid twentieth century. There were other groups like the Woodcraft Folk (which has a New Age sound about it) but these never seem to be identifiably represented on postcards. All in all no youth movement of any kind currently shows its head above ground, at least in my part of London. There was also a world of work exemplified by hotel bellboys (16.*vi*, 16.*vii*, 16.*viii*) and Post Office telegraph boys. Even choristers could be said to wear uniforms though they inhabit a category of their own.

I graduated to the Scouts but did not persevere. I thought I had said goodbye to uniforms but was briefly roped in at school to the wretched Air Training Corps which just seemed to march round and round the building. I swore never to wear a uniform again and now don't even own a suit.

16.ii

16.iii Baxter's, Hinckley

16.iv

16.v

16.vi Cinema Studios, Tooting

16.vii Horace Dudley, Photographic Artist, Stoke

16.viii W. H. Broad, Bournemouth

16.ix

16.x Phillips, East Stow

16.xi

16.xii

16.xiii

16.xiv J. W. Rogers, Day & Electric Studio, Wellingborough

16.xv Palace Studios, Halifax

16.xvi National Photo Co.

16.xvii

16.xviii

16.xix

Maternity

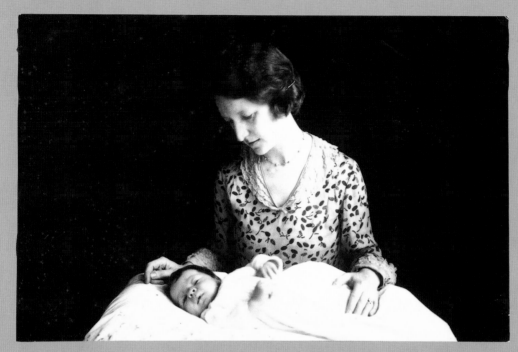

17.i

The image of maternity has a long history. The icon of the Madonna and Child is central to Christian art and its echoes haunt many of these portraits. It is easy to spot those made with the Old Masters in mind from Bellini to Rubens. In the real world however the squirming or changes of expression of a young baby cannot be regulated and attempts by the mother at producing a Raphaelesque unity of mood and physical alignment often go awry. In *17.ix* the idea of *contrapposto* is taken an uncomfortable twist too far. On the other hand *17.x* and *17.xi* have an almost Flemish simplicity and directness brought to an even more tender combination of limbs and expression in the picture above. Other more informal glimpses of beauty can come out of such a visit to the photographer's studio where this tenderest of relationships may happily record itself. Love and wonder can momentarily transform the face of the plainest mother.

The interior bedroom scene is a rarity and in *17.ii* is achieved in natural indoor light by an intrepid amateur photographer. Since this is probably the father a new dimension is added to a doting theme. Pictures of mother and baby are proof against fashion and it is quite unusual to find total failure, although *17.xiv* manages to convey an atmosphere of gothic gloom.

One subtle difference between these and other pictures of women early in the twentieth century is the absence of hats. The stiffly formal presentation of *17.xii* is an unusual and rather bleak exception.

Part of the premise which guides this project is that any theme is illuminated by repetition through its possible variations. That of mother and very young baby shows a (literal) no man's land between pregnancy and motherhood where one flesh has become two but the act of separation is still far from complete.

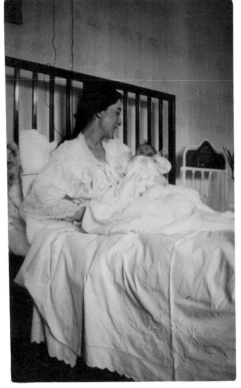

17.ii 1920

17.iii

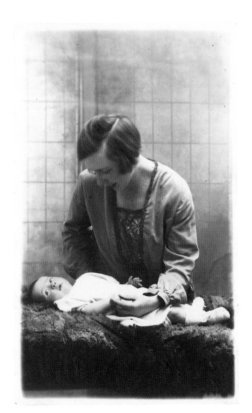

17.iv

17.v W. T. Munns, Gravesend

17.vi

17.vii

17.viii 1917

17.ix 1921

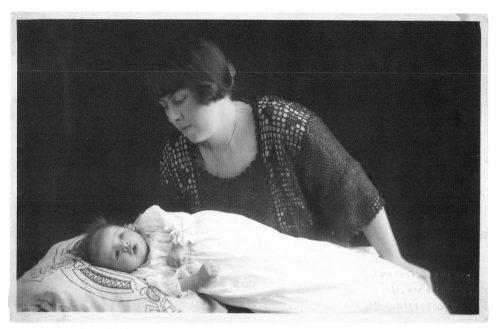

17.x Parisian Studios, Gillingham

17.xi F. K. Evitt, Vandyk Studio, Farnborough

17.xii

17.xiii

17.xiv

17.xv Electric Light Studio, Daygate, York

17.xvi

Prizewinners

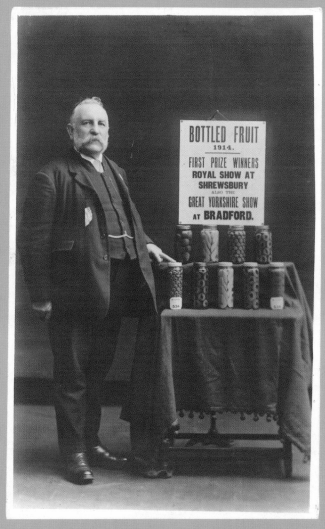

18.i 1914 A. E. Ball, Stockton

Stand by your prize is the regular formula here. Some, however, prefer to pose with the victorious beast or product, as is the case with my own prize for prizewinners, awarded to the above not only for his spectacular display of bottled fruit but for his poise and bravado. A fireman cannot of course pose with a fire nor an athlete with a race and it is difficult in those cases where no clue is given (whether it be gun or rabbit or violin) to find out what the proud guardian of a cup or shield has done. The very gleam of mirror-polished silver makes the reading of inscriptions difficult.

The level of award does not seem to matter. From the man who wins a pipe and a print for dressing in a suit made from the lids of shoe polish tins (*18.v*) to the heroes whose exploits gain them cascades of cutlery, clocks, barometers and biscuit barrels (*18.iii*), all present themselves to be photographed.

Many set out their display in the garden or prepare a makeshift background, presumably because of the difficulty of transporting (in the case of the Eisteddfod champion, *18.xvi*) several heavy chairs and a forest of trophies.

There seems to be no human activity for which some sort of prize is not there to be won, though I guess it's a long time since anyone (least of all a plump white girl) claimed the Cake Walk Cup.

18.ii

18.iii

18.iv

18.v

18.vi

18.vii 1905

18.viii

18.ix William's Pioneer Studios Ltd,
London & Provinces

18.x J. Vaughan Evans & Sons, Llanelly

18.xi

18.xii 1918

18.xiii Vaudeville Studios, East Ham

18.xiv

18.xv J. Campbell Harper, Leith

18.xvi 1932

18.xvii

Tinted Cards

19.i H. Dalton, Chorley

Tinting was a service offered by most studios but few customers took advantage of it judging by the surviving proportion of tinted cards. Even in the 1930s, the heyday of tinting, barely half a percent of studio portrait sitters opted for tuppence coloured rather than penny plain. The only exceptions were the head-and-shoulders portrait cards of schoolchildren (see Introduction, *fig. 10*) which feature in another category. Now and then one comes across a real colour photograph such as *19.vi* (it can be difficult to tell) although these are a rarity.

The best professional tinting is refined and very accomplished with skilful blends for the flesh (*19.xvi* is a perfect example) but it was not long before DIY moved in and sets of rather acidic tinting colours could be bought at the chemist's shop. They were quite difficult to use, especially if one lacked proper sable brushes. My own efforts aged ten or so were no less catastrophic than the worst of those illustrated here. Though many of these seem fairly wild they were sometimes oddly prophetic of certain of the isms of modern art. Andy Warhol in his early years was greatly fascinated by tinted photos and their special versions of reality.

Ladies fare better than men it would appear, but it must be remembered that the commercially tinted photos of 1930s film stars show men with highly made up and seemingly lipsticked faces.

The serviceman with pyramids (*19.xiv*) who has taken photos of his wife and child to the photographer in Cairo is a fine example of pre-Photoshop wizardry.

19.ii 1934 Jerome Ltd

19.iii 1933 Jerome Ltd

19.iv 1934 Jerome Ltd

19.v

19.vi

19.vii

19.viii 1932 Jerome Ltd

19.ix Gale's Studios, Manchester

19.x

19.xi Jerome Ltd

19.xii Mrs John Martin & Son, Poplar

19.xiii 1930 Eastbourne Photo Co., Clapham

19.xiv V Studio Art, Cairo

19.xv

19.xvi London Studios, Moseley

19.xvii J. H. Jamieson, Nelson

19.xviii

19.xix

Infant Fashion Girls

20.i 1907

We only know that the flounced little figure above is a girl from the inscription on the back. She is Ethel but it would have been no surprise to find that she was a he and called Bertie for no differentiation was made for the first few years of life. The smarter unisex child wore clothing almost as complicated as that of the female adult. In the case of girls occasional specialisation came when they were dressed as miniature women, sporting a huge hat and fur trimmed coat with matching muff and shiny boots (*20.viii, 20.xi*).

Many of these infants whether under direction from adults or through some as yet undiscovered hardwiring seem effortlessly to slide into grown up poses as in *20.xiii*.

What these cards are free of (and what poisons almost all commercial cards featuring small children) is a knowing cuteness of expression. Such early ruin of innocence makes innocence itself a theatrical quality to be acted out.

No concession is made to infancy in terms of background. They are dumped against the usual baronial interiors or plonked on a papier-mâché balustrade in front of a pastoral vista (*20.xi*) or stood next to or on top of pieces of furniture made for giants (*20.viii*).

20.ii Barcham

20.iii

20.iv

20.v

20.vi F. G. Brewis, Newcastle on Tyne

20.vii USA Studios

20.viii

20.ix

20.x

20.xi Fred Quinton, Newport, I.O.W.

20.xii 1928 Buckley Studios, Bolton

20.xiii Angle Photographer, Walworth Rd

20.xiv A. J. Cross, Whitchurch, Salop

20.xv

20.xvi J. Harrison, Imperial Studio, Nelson

20.xvii

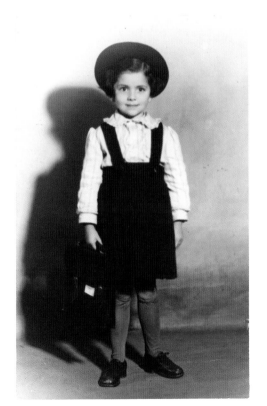

20.xviii

20.xix

Readers

The largely silent act of reading suits the postcard well though literature came to be a standard studio prop to prevent restlessness. In nine cases out of ten the book being read earnestly or wistfully, or with smiling delight, in the studio is a back issue of *The Camera Year* or *Photographers' Monthly*.

The lady with the classic Penguin above is not however going to be distracted as she reaches the last few climactic pages of a Dorothy L. Sayers whodunit. Purposive reading is more likely to be of newspapers and periodicals whether *The People* (read to an audience of dolls in *21.ii*), or *Film Fun* (an idle comic for an apparently idle hour) or Pearson's magazine (*21.iii*) read outside the tent. Mother or grandmother reading or seeming to read to children is a familiar trope (*21.vi*, *21.viii*) and clergymen like to be observed with the Word that they preach, rhetorically held open (*21.vii*).

Perhaps the purest of reading poses is sustained by *21.x* immersed in a folio as the steamer ploughs on while others catch the sun on deck. If the lady with the *Daily Mail* (*21.xv*) seems easily diverted from her newspaper by the photographer she has every excuse if we look at the uninviting headline, 'Essolube – The triumph of Hydrogenation'.

21.ii Jerome Ltd

21.iii

21.iv

21.v

21.vi 1910

21.vii

21.viii

21.ix C. H. Deakin, Newcastle, Staffs

21.x

21.xi

21.xii

21.xiii

21.xiv

21.xv Henry Chapman, Swansea

Women in Uniform War Workers

22.i 1917 Paul Coe, Gloucester

Nothing accelerated the political advancement of women so much as the need for workers in wartime, both for the extraordinary demands of war itself (munitions, medicine etc.) and to replace in field and factory the increasingly absent and unreturning men. The old cover was blown as definitive proof was given of women's capabilities. The arduousness of domestic toil was as good a preparation as any for the hardships of factory life.

The real mould breakers amongst the civilian workers were those in the great munitions factories who were unprecedentedly paid a wage comparable to that of a man. Pride in the new trousered uniform is apparent and the triangular badges of the Women Volunteers are often seen. The uniform of the Land Army was a cause of ribaldry when it first appeared though one woman at least (22.xii) shows how dashing a version was possible. Such tailored moments of understandable vanity were soon forgotten once the work itself began, as one can see in 22.xxxi. The Land Girl in 22.xxxix, now truly broken in, once perhaps sported a fashion plate outfit as fresh as that of 22.xiv. In the studio portraits although the women have undergone a revolution in dress the backgrounds remain the same with their accustomed props. Even the traditional poses (now not quite as convincing with posture and position of legs less voluminously concealed) tend to be maintained.

22.ii

22.iii Relph & Co., 130 Church St, Preston

22.iv

22.v Percy J. Sansom, Doncaster

22.vi

22.vii

22.viii

22.ix

22.x Gale's Studios

22.xi W. Wills, 250 High Road, S. Tottenham

22.xii Leek

22.xiii Stafford

22.xiv 1916

22.xv H. Hearne, Folkestone

22.xvi Leeds

22.xvii

22.xviii Swindon

22.xix 1919

22.xx Louise M. Smith, Newport, Mon.

22.xxi

206

22.xxii James Dewar, Glasgow

22.xxiii Stacey Ward Studios, Willesden

22.xxiv H. Tewson, Leeds

22.xxv Dura Ltd

22.xxvi

22.xxvii Sharpe's Studio, Canning Town

22.xxviii

22.xxix A. & G. Taylor, 62 Market Street, Manchester

22.xxx Van Ralty, Manchester

22.xxxi S. Yorks

22.xxxii

22.xxxiii Van Ralty

22.xxxiv J. H. Jamieson, Preston

22.xxxv P. Higdon, Street, Somerset

22.xxxvi

22.xxxvii Broxby, Bishops Stortford

22.xxxviii S. J. Priest, Barrow in Furness

22.xxxix

The Garden Gardening

23.*i*

The garden was one of the first areas where the serious (and the later more cavalier) amateur photographer could compete on almost equal terms with the professional. Open daylight allowed for more generous apertures and faster shutter speeds, while gardens themselves embodied an aesthetic of the picturesque full of already arranged compositional artifice.

The garden portrait (a category in its own right not featured here) was originally the province of the itinerant street photographer and it is only when the amateur takes over that we routinely see scenes of actual gardening. Pseudo gardening is a more common subject with much feigned picking and sniffing of

flowers: in *23.x* we see an expert demonstration of this by a lady who, judging from her hat with its hanging ties, will soon be off in a motor car. Rougher aspects of the gardener's toil were of course, in the more ample gardens, largely performed by staff or hirelings. These in the egalitarian world of the postcard portrait also may have their day and even the garden's owner may later allow himself to be caught at work, eventually with pride.

Central Casting, which so often comes up trumps in this book, has evidently produced both the gardener and housekeeper in *23.ix*, as well as the gardener's boy plus maids in *23.xi*.

23.ii

23.iii

23.iv

23.v

23.vi The City Studio, Durham

23.vii

23.viii

23.ix

23.x

23.xi

23.xii

23.xiii

23.xiv

School the Classroom

24.i 1910

The day the school photographer arrives is still a ritual event, the classic result of which continues to be that long group photograph which every luckless parent buys for the small blob that is their child. My young stepchildren still have individual school portraits done, no longer as postcards of course but as presentation photos in digital colour. The playground continues to be the arena for the general photograph while a special booth is set up as a studio for the portraits.

The classroom view had a shorter vogue yet it gives an intimate glimpse of schoolchildren in their own environment. The setting is largely the standard classroom of schools that were built around 1906, in the great expansion that followed the Education Act. In order to take advantage of the main source of light the children are often squeezed into one half of the room. They frequently show examples of work like the stiff drawings of plants copied from some slightly less stiff original in an age before the dawn of self-expression.

Occasionally as in *24.xiii* one sees a pose unknown today called 'sitting to attention' where the arms are folded behind a straight back. Infant schools seldom seem as formal though even the floor can manage to divide itself into rigid rows (*24.vi*).

The teacher is often featured. He or she usually stands at the back looking serious though surely the figure in an Eton collar posing effetely in front of the Euclidean solids (*24.ii*) is a prefect.

24.ii

24.iii

24.iv J. G. Taylor, London N.

24.v

24.vi

24.vii

24.viii

24.ix

24.x

222

24.xi

24.xii

24.xiii G. S. Gantry, Bowes Park

24.xiv 1930

24.xv

24.xvi

Fantasy Transport the Aeroplane

25.i

Fantasy aeroplanes (and even the baskets of sedate balloonists) are invariably three-dimensional contraptions with the lower parts of the fliers' bodies concealed. It is one of the puzzles of all such cards to assess the degree to which these now primitive-seeming arrangements corresponded to what today we call virtual reality. Certainly some of the fantasy pilots take themselves rather seriously.

Most of these photographs were taken in seaside towns where England's first air displays were organised. Blackpool was early off the mark with regular aviation spectacles from 1909, only a year after the Wright brothers' first public demonstration of controlled flight.

The early planes were as sketchy as their studio equivalents but the pace of aeronautic development was hard to keep up with. One of the more successful of later simulations (25.xvii) has a stylish occupant who looks ready to take on Amy Johnson herself.

A rare late contender from the Second World War (25.xvi) is a fully armed fighter plane (marked 'British Bomber') flying over a Berlin that features swastikas, shell bursts and plummeting German aircraft. It marks the end of a forty-year road of simulated flight and seems a long way from the lads with backturned caps (in imitation of a style set by Wilbur Wright) who took off into the studio skies.

25.ii

25.iii

25.iv

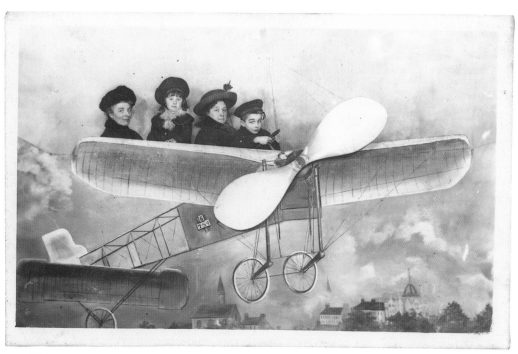

25.v 1910

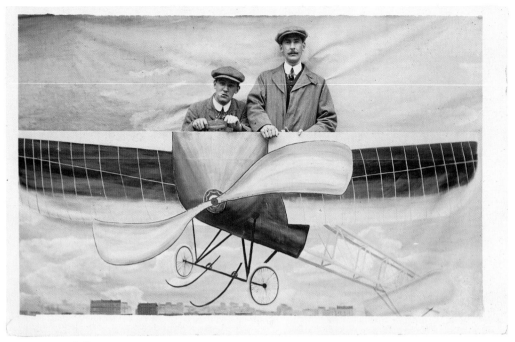

25.*vi* Lees, Portobello

25.*vii* J. G. Brown & Co., Montrose

25.viii

25.ix

25.x J. F. Ballantyne, Weston S. Mare

25.xi

25.xii

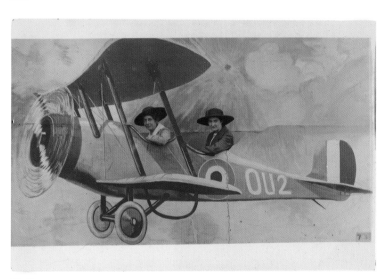

25.xiii

25.xiv

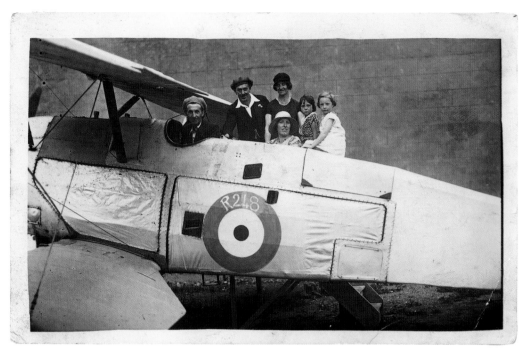

25.xv

25.xvi

25.xvii

Shops

26.i

A shop from another era is always fascinating and the ultimate pleasure of the seated *flaneur* is to go window shopping in the past. As with people so with shops and there can hardly have been a corner store that did not have its own postcard; even the nameless shop in *26.viii* that sold next to nothing. Shops of course took care to dress for photography and to assert their uptodateness. Dealers in the second hand were a natural exception and it is odd that the chairs outside *26.xxxiv* are exactly the kind you will see in front of even a modest junk shop today. In their displays and announcements of bargains shops could be as raucous and dazzling as their current counterparts. Nor were they coy: a butcher's shop was a no nonsense demonstration of where meat comes from.

Modern sensibilities would find the display in *26.xi* rather challenging. Paradoxically it is also a butcher's shop that provides in *26.x* the most poetic of these images, caught in the raking light of a summer evening.

Postcards of shop interiors have a special flavour and are much rarer. It is difficult to work out what is going on in the waxwork-like dress shop (*26.xx*) but three gentlemen are waiting to sell you the identical hat in *26.xxi*. The newsagent, like the above or one of the rapidly expanding W.H. Smith chain (*26.xxvi*), will tell you among other things what day it is by virtue of their placards announcing the activities of Suffragettes or the Greeks or Mr Balfour.

26.ii

26.iii

26.iv 1915 Herbert Pearson, Crewe

26.v

26.vi 1920 Star Photographic Co., London SE1

26.vii

26.viii

26.ix

26.x

26.xi

238

26.xii

26.xiii

26.xiv

26.xv

26.xvi

26.xvii

26.xviii

26.xix

26.xx

26.xxi

26.xxii

26.xxiii

26.xxiv

26.xxv

26.xxvi

26.xxvii

26.xxviii

26.xxix

26.xxx

26.xxxi

26.xxxii

26.xxxiii

26.xxxiv

26.xxxv

Sport

27.i 1908

One could hardly have a more archetypal footballer than this man and, since football is now the year-round dominant sport in the world, his emblematic figure rightly begins this group of images. Even an extended selection cannot cover the whole spectrum of sporting activity but I am pleased (considering the infrequency of postcard representations) to be able to include ping-pong, the sport of artists, intellectuals and Jewish novelists. What is more the picture features a bulky chap playing before an audience of admiring women. Women themselves are well represented and although the iconic footballer is mandatory the most elegant performer is the amazing woman ice-skater in *27.vi*, who achieves a moment of visual perfection. The lady cricketers are unlikely to be able to steal a quick single in their long skirts but it is more surprising to see that women actually played tennis in those hats (*27.iii*) and did so with some verve. I do not know exactly what sport *27.xix* represents but he is certainly in good shape for it, just as the capped and blazered gentleman in *27.xxxii* represents all the poise and confidence of a sportsman of distinction.

One image that captures the complete absorption that sport demands returns us to football (*27.xxiv*). All eyes are on the ball and each player is assessing his move should it come his way. The studio photographer on the other hand does not always quite convey the flavour of a sport and one finds it baffling to see the runners in *27.xxv* all geared up to race across the room.

27.ii

27.iii

27.iv

27.v 1910

27.vi

27.vii 1908

27.viii

27.ix

27.x

27.xi

27.xii

27.xiii L. Vautier, Bristol

27.xiv

27.xv

27.xvi 1947 Columbia Studios, London N17

27.xvii

27.xviii S. Harrison

27.xix

27.xx

27.xxi

27.xxii H. Mumford, Wallasey

27.xxiii

27.xxiv

27.xxv

27.xxvi

27.xxvii

27.xxviii

27.xxix E. Maplesden Young, Deal

27.xxx

27.xxxi

27.xxxii

27.xxxiii

27.xxxiv

Two Women Actuality

28.i

Having looked now at thousands of pictures either involving two men or two women I sense a difference in attitude and approach. Two men seem less likely to invent special selves for the studio photographer and are far less likely to prepare in advance for the encounter. Their outdoor and indoor selves, their public and private personalities, diverge far less than those of women. Thus Two Women becomes a pair of categories which I have labelled Studio and Actuality. To indulge in another generalisation I cannot resist the impression that two women thus seen together have in some way *escaped*. Men are also prisoners of course, in the earlier part of the century especially, of stifling conventions of dress and behaviour but these are often the trappings and the suits of power.

Both groups however, presented as pairs, offer the same challenge of guessing at their relationships. As with men one does not know whether these women are close relatives, colleagues, friends, or lovers. The two women above have a classic bond impossible to distinguish in other circumstances: they are neighbours. This may indeed be an invisible factor that brings many such couples together on holiday or on shopping trips. Are the two ancient ladies in *28.xxvi* (also divided by a fence) their equivalents born two generations before?

28.ii

28.iii

28.iv

28.v

28.vi

28.vii

28.viii

28.ix

28.x 1912 Worcester

28.xi 1934 Sunbeam Photo Ltd, Margate

28.xii

28.xiii

28.xiv The Metaline Co., Tottenham

28.xv

28.xvi Jerome Ltd

28.xvii

28.xviii

28.xix

28.xx Empire Films, Clacton on Sea

28.xxi Bride's Holiday Postcards, Clevedon

28.xxii

28.xxiii

28.xxiv

28.xxv

28.xxvi

Boats

29.i 1917

I know nothing about boats. I have however experienced that riverine pleasure presented above when the wind is in the willows and the sun turns water into gold. Such rapture in the dappled and lazy world of purposeless boating is also captured in *29.ii* and *29.iv*. All else speaks to me of blisters and sore arms or the near fatal swing of a boom.

Yachting is shown here only in token form (*29.xvii*) where one boat is launched from another. Pictures of yachts seem poetic only at a distance where the yachtsperson is a mere dot. Images where a boat expresses the water, even though it is not the most prominent feature, are especially telling as in *29.xiv*, *29.xv* and *29.xviii*, each a composition of some elegance.

None of the boats is going far except the liner bound for Cape Town (*29.xxiii*) with its thoughtful passengers many of whom are heading for a new life. The other large vessels are for trippers who have already fallen for the idea of a group photograph before their excursion around the bay. If the day is not fine some may end up like the numb figure on the deck in *29.xxiv*, a scene of queasy desolation serving to remind me that I prefer to go to sea in a book, preferably in the company of Joseph Conrad.

29.ii 1912

29.iii

29.iv

29.v

29.vi

29.vii

29.viii Jerome Ltd

29.ix

29.x 1934 Sunny Snaps, Worthing

29.xi

29.xii

29.xiii

29.xiv Jerome Ltd, Kings Cross

29.xv

29.xvi

29.xvii Jackson's Faces

29.xviii

29.xix Jackson's Faces, G. Yarmouth

29.xx

29.xxi 1907

29.xxii

29.xxiii 1920

29.xxiv 1919 Crossing to Ireland

Man and Child

30.i

Woman and Child seemed a natural category from the outset as I decided what core samplings to make of the huge amount of material I was gathering. But, as with the Aspidistra, categories emerge of their own accord. Some of these remained small while others piled up steadily. The fact that Man and Child did not occur to me initially is itself symptomatic of prejudicial error. Most of these are, one supposes, pictures of fathers with their children and they have their own quite different poetry from those involving the mother. The man has his own particular fragments of time with his children, grandchildren or nieces and can be a valued companion of adventure or anarchic playfulness. There can be a

special and secret dialogue that a child establishes with a senior male in the family.

This combination of aspects comes out in the photographic postcard which somehow acts as a neutral observer of bonds simultaneously very robust and intimately fragile. What is unsaid in *30.vi* and *30.xi* seems to have its own eloquence and there is always a necessarily unstated situation between the serving soldier and his children, a mood perfectly caught in *30.viii*.

Men are seldom convincing however (at least at this period) as baby carriers; their moment will come.

30.ii 1930 Margate

30.iii 1920 Margate

30.iv Jerome Ltd

30.v Geo. Austin, Eastbourne

30.vi

30.vii

30.viii L. Dunn, Shildon

30.ix

30.x Ipswich

30.xi

30.xii

30.xiii

30.xiv 1932 J. Roberts, Leeds

30.xv Fox's Studios, Edgware

30.xvi

30.xvii Sunbeam Photo Ltd, Margate

30.xviii 1911 The Hudson Studios, Birmingham

30.xix

30.xx H. H. Dudley, West Bromwich

30.xxi 1926 Coldham & Son, Northampton

Women in Fashion 1920s and 1930s

31.i 1928 Bradley & Evans,
Colchester

Those historians who regard the twentieth century as a short one, beginning with the First World War and ending with the fall of the Berlin Wall, could well have described its start with what we might now call a radical makeover of the idea of a woman. This accompanied great political events and the change effected in a couple of decades was as much a break with tyranny as any great political shift.

When it came to women and fashion the pile of cards grew higher and higher. Whereas male costume occupied a narrow world with a slow story line, women's fashion reflected and embodied each twist and turn of the

century's narrative. Subdivisions became a necessity, although separating categories by period is perilous. I suspect that costume historians ignore in their own datelines the difference between London and the provinces, and the clothes worn by older and younger women, to mention only two of the many variables that make nonsense of mechanical time schemes.

Here is a small fashion parade across two decades. The only commentary needed is to point out that it is not only high fashion that is on view but what people actually wore, which includes that which they made themselves.

31.ii

31.iii 1934 Jerome Ltd

31.iv Jerome Ltd

31.v 1935

31.vi 1932 Jerome Ltd

31.vii 1936 Dyke Bros

31.viii 1934

31.ix 1931

31.x Jerome Ltd

31.xi 1927 J. G. Bullen, Grimsby

31.xii

31.xiii 1935

31.xiv Empire Studios

31.xv Jerome Ltd

31.xvi 1936

31.xvii 1929 Pictorial Studios, Sunderland

31.xviii Jerome Ltd

31.xix H. H. Wragg

31.xx Mower's Studio, Bath

31.xxi 1927 Claude Cross, Norwich

Charabancs

32.i A. Glover,
Portsmouth

The motor charabanc took over gradually from the horse-driven version though both initially reflected the original significance of the French word meaning cart-with-benches. The solid tyres and spartan seating of early models, bumping along roads as yet without tarmac, must have led to rides more braced against than bracing.

Some coaches were merely the ancestors of the stretch limo but the great leviathans, such as those we see ranged above with their drivers, could hold thirty or more people. This was good news for the postcard photographer (who took his shot at the outset of the trip and had the cards ready for purchase on the return to base).

At their height, with a public who would have had no other means of visiting well known beauty spots, charabancs were big business. Rival firms touted their excursions at the beach or on the street. Women's fashion soon adjusted to life at 12mph (the regulation speed) and smaller hats did not need to be tied down with ribbons.

Gradually this trade diminished with the growth of the private car. Indeed coach trips acquired a bad reputation as works' outings became little more than motorised pub crawls. By the end of the 1930s the notice 'No Coaches or Charabancs' was commonly seen outside the more dignified roadside inns.

32.ii

32.iii 1922

32.iv

32.v

32.vi

32.vii

32.viii

32.ix

32.x 1922 Windsor

32.xi

32.xii   1932

32.xiii

32.xiv

32.xv Walker, Teignmouth

Dolls

33.i
A. & G. Taylor,
Cardiff

These are the human aristocrats of the doll world.
Animals and cuddly indeterminables have categories
to themselves, together with that star of dolls, the
Teddy Bear. Occasionally a doll might be resident at
the photographer's studio but the majority are the
child's own proud possessions. Mostly these dolls are
of the classic type you see now in auction catalogued
as German-made rarities with astonishing estimated
prices. Here, unaware of their future value, they play
their not entirely subservient roles in these children's
lives as companions or surrogate babies or comforting
guardians.

Their dress is usually elaborate, often more elaborate
than that of the children who present them or wheel

them around, or show them in the context of a dolls'
house or, as above, in a customised bed.

Boys also had dolls to comfort them at bedtime but did
not like so much to be seen out with them, nor wanted all
the paraphernalia of prams and dolls' clothes. Their dolls
were more often characters, such as clowns and soldiers
or the golliwog in 33.vi, representing the same divide as
persists now between Barbie dolls and Action Men.

Even dolls that blink and wink and are fully articulated
tend to stare blankly out but a child reads worlds of
emotion into their indifference, as can be seen in 33.xvi
where, as if on a darkened stage, the emotional drama
of child and doll is acted out.

33.ii Casterton

33.iii

33.iv

33.v Belfast

33.vi 1926 Tontine, Folkestone

33.vii Dura Ltd

33.viii H. Bentley, Barrow-in-Furness

33.ix 1930 Empire Studios

33.x Emberson Jno, Tooting

33.xi

33.xii Happy Snaps, Blackpool

33.xiii

33.xiv

33.xv

33.xvi J. Perkoff, N.E. London

Bicycles

34.i 1935
Richmond,
Yorks

Of all possessions that people liked to have themselves pictured with the bicycle was king. Naturally the gleaming new machine is proudly shown off but the well worn and trusty friend is equally paraded.

Both for men and women in the earlier years of the century the cycle symbolised independence and broader horizons. For women it had a special role on the bumpy and furrowed road to emancipation. It provided a wonderful alibi for unchaperoned adventure even though most early women cyclists seem still to be encumbered by clothing that made riding difficult as well as hats of immeasurable unsuitability. I would not have predicted at the outset of this enterprise that the proportion of women to men photographed with their bicycles would turn out to be anywhere near seventy per cent (derived from a sampling of more than a thousand cards).

Cycling groups in carefree mood escape like supercharged ramblers to fresh fields and new circles of acquaintance. The spirit of these early cyclists is well described by H.G. Wells and many of his Mr Pollys are here.

I can't myself help identifying with the boys in 34.xvii though slightly afraid I might be the swat with the binoculars. Much of my schoolday cycling life is in this picture, as indeed the photograph above reminds me of my shortlived membership of the Cyclists' Touring Club, here seen heading for Richmond in 1935. Things had not changed by 1954 when after a similarly damp outing I decided to quit. The Tooting Bec branch of the CTC did not feature women such as 34.iii, the Ingrid Bergman of the bike, or the come hither seductress waiting behind the shed in 34.xxv.

34.ii

34.iii

34.iv

34.v Leicestershire

34.vi

34.vii J. Steele, Breckin

34.viii Kidderminster

34.ix

34.x Ambleside

34.xi

34.xii

34.xiii Jerome Ltd

34.xiv

34.xv

34.xvi

34.xvii Alex. H. Low

34.xviii Gale & Polden

34.xix 1907

34.xx

34.xxi

34.xxii Scotland

34.xxiii Frank Bailey, Canterbury

34.xxiv

34.xxv

34.xxvi

34.xxvii

34.xxviii

Soldiers Portraits

35.i 1917

Those versed in badge and uniform would be able to identify the regiments and rank of these soldiers but such is not the argument of this selection of representative army servicemen.

Portraiture here has a special imperative since, for so many soldiers, these pictures would be their last. Moreover, their very anonymity makes this, statistically, a grimly calculable matter.

Many are pictured at that moment of pride when they first acquired their uniform. The sheer number of equivalent portraits (as well as the more general full-length and group shots that make up other categories) suggests that almost every serviceman had such a

memento to leave with a loved one or post off to a friend.

The studio postcard portrait was already in decline by the Second World War though *35.ii* demonstrates that it was still possible to enter a photographer's shop and emerge with a fine picture; in this case perhaps the finest in terms of lighting, mood and composition.

Any large camp like Catterick in Yorkshire would have a photographer and a fair proportion of these portraits were taken on active service or return from leave. Occasionally behind their would-be confident gaze is a shudder of fear in the new recruit or a numbness that suggests that those who have returned from the front have seen horrors that will haunt them forever.

35.ii Richmond, Yorks

35.iii

35.iv Modern Studios, Leeds

35.v

35.vi 1917 E. A. Osborne, Falmouth

35.vii

35.viii

35.ix Van Ralty, Manchester

35.x Hovel Studio, Alexandria

35.xi

35.xii Dixon Studios Ltd, Southend

35.xiii 1914

35.xiv

35.xv Glasgow

35.xvi Derby

35.xvii Folkestone

35.xviii

35.xix Manchester

35.xx J.J. Payne's Studio

35.xxi Manchester

35.xxii Derby

35.xxiii

35.xxiv

35.xxv Clacton

35.xxvi 1916 Nottingham

35.xxvii South Shields

35.xxviii Southport

35.xxix 1914 Withernsea

35.xxx Hungerford

35.xxxi

35.xxxii

35.xxxiii Richmond, Yorks

35.xxxiv Coventry

Bathers

36.i

Bathers come in all shapes and sizes and in all kinds of groups including the massed aquatic gathering of which *36.iii* is typical (another opportunity for the beach photographer to bump up his sales) as is *36.xvi* which includes the mass fad of the time, the synchronised 'thumbs up' sign.

This selection can hardly avoid becoming a parade of changing habits in beachwear. The great paradox of Edwardian seaside costume is that its effortful modesty as body covering was contradicted by its explicit revelation of anatomical detail when wet. The observant child would have known more about mammary variety and male genitalia than my more repressed generation was able to imagine.

Saucier but less revealing were the commercial cards (mostly printed in France which was synonymous with naughtiness) that featured models dressed, as time moved on from the early years of the century, with progressive scantiness. Pictures of a man's girlfriend taken in emulation of these (*36.xiii*, *36.xviii* and *36.xix*) were the last word in daring. The image of three generations of the family bathing together in *36.xvii* is especially touching since the oldest of the group would have bathed as a young girl in the full flounced outfit of the Edwardian era while the youngest might have lived to walk the topless beaches of today.

36.ii 1909 Folkestone

36.iii

36.iv

36.v Douglas, I.O.M.

36.vi

36.vii Doran, Royal Photographer, Filey

36.viii

36.ix

36.x

36.xi

36.xii Sunbeam Photos Ltd, Margate

36.xiii

36.xiv 1914

36.xv

36.xvi

36.xvii

36.xviii

36.xix

Select Bibliography

H.W.K. Collam, *Come Autumn Hand* (1943)

Michael Willoughby, *A History of Postcards* (Studio Editions, London, 1972)

T. and V. Holt, *Till the Boys Come Home: Picture Postcards of World War 1* (MacDonald & James, London, 1977)

Jaap Boerdam and Warna Oosterbaan Martinius, Netherlands Journal of Sociology, 16, 1980

Gisèle Freund, *Photography and Society* (Gordon Fraser, London, 1980 [1974])

Julia Hirsch, *Family Photographs: Content, Meaning and Effect* (New York University Press, 1981)

Pat Holland and Jo Spence (eds), *Family Snaps: On the Meaning of Domestic Photography* (Virago, London, 1991)

Raphael Samuel, *People's History and Socialist Theory* (Routledge and Kegan Paul, London, 1981)

A. Linkman and C. Warhurst, *Family Albums* (Manchester Studies Series, 1982)

Roland Barthes, *Camera Lucida* (Flamingo, London, 1984)

Erving Goffmann, *The Presentation of Self in Everyday Life* (Penguin, London, 1990 [1959])

Pierre Bourdieu, *Photography: A Middle Brow Art* (Polity Press, Cambridge, 1990)

Richard Brilliant, *Portraiture* (Reaktion, London, 1991)

G. Clarke, *The Portrait in Photography* (Reaktion, London, 1992)

Nikolas Rose, *Inventing Ourselves: Psychology, Power and Personhood* (Cambridge University Press, 1996)

J. Woodall (ed.), *Portraiture: Facing the Subject* (Manchester University Press, 1997)

Marianne Hirsch, *Family Frames: Photography, Narrative and Postmemory* (Harvard University Press, Massachusetts, 1997)

Libby Hall, *Prince and Other Dogs* (Bloomsbury USA, New York, 2000)

Tom Phillips, *The Postcard Century* (Thames & Hudson, London, 2000)

Martha Langford, *Suspended Conversations* (McGill-Queens University Press, Montreal, 2001)

Robert Pols, *Family Photographs 1860–1945* (Public Record Office, London, 2002)

Elizabeth Edwards and Janice Hart (eds), *Photographs Objects Histories* (Routledge, London, 2004)

Index

References in *italics* are to illustrations